The Path To Guidance

Ibn Qayyim al-Jawziyyah

Copyright

Ibn Qayyim al-Jawziyyah
Editor Imam Ahamd
El-Farouq.org

The Text of the Treatise

In the Name of Allaah, Full of Mercy,
Ever-Merciful to His (Believing) Servants

(1) This is a book which the Shaikh, the Imaam, the 'Allaamah, the Shaikh of Islaam and the Muftee of the Muslims, Aboo 'Abdullaah Muhammad the son of Aboo Bakr - better known as Ibn Qayyim al-Jawziyyah - may Allaah the Exalted have mercy upon him, sent to one of his brothers. He said:

BLESSING LIES IN GIVING ADVICE AND TEACHING

(2) "Allaah is the One I ask and for Whose reply I hope: that He is benevolent to the brother in this life and the hereafter, that He brings about benefit by him and makes him blessed wherever he may be. Verily the blessing of a man lies in his teaching of goodness wherever he may be and his giving of advice to everyone he meets. Allaah, the Exalted said, informing about al-Maseeh (i.e., Jesus) (ʋ):

And He made me blessed wherever I may be. [Soorah Maryam (19):31].

Meaning, 'A teacher of goodness, a caller to Allaah, one who reminds (others) of Him and who exhorts them to His obedience.' So this is from the blessing of a man.

(3) Whoever is devoid of these (characteristics) is devoid of blessing and so the blessing of meeting such a person and spending time with him is removed. In fact, the blessing of the one who meets him and spends time with him will also be removed if he should waste time in merely talking about occurrences and events, thus corrupting the heart. [refer to the chapter one: The Sound Heart]

(4) Every harm that enters upon a servant, is caused by the heart's corruption. The corruption of the heart in turn brings about the removal of the heart's right upon Allaah, the Exalted, and a diminution of its degree and rank in the sight of Allaah. For this reason, some of the shaikhs advised with their saying, "Be cautious of (the) mixing with a person which will cause wastage of time and corruption of the heart. For verily, when time is wasted and the heart is corrupted, all of the affairs of the servant will become ruined,[1] `and he will be of those about whom Allaah, the Exalted, said:

And obey not him whose heart We have made heedless of Our Remembrance, one who follows his own lusts and whose affair has been lost and wasted. [Soorah al-Kahf (18):28].

THE PUNISHMENT FOR HEEDLESSNESS

(5) Whoever reflects upon the nature and the state of creation will find that, excepting a very small number, all of them are of those whose hearts are unmindful of the remembrance of Allaah, the Exalted; those who have followed their desires and whose affairs and well-being have become a ruin. This means that they have neglected what will benefit them and bring about their well-being. They occupy themselves with what does not benefit them - rather, with what brings harm upon them in this life and the next.

(6) It is such people that Allaah, free from all imperfection, ordered His Messenger not to obey. Obedience to the Messenger cannot be perfected unless obedience is denied to such people, because they call only to that which causes difficulties and hardships, such as following desires and being heedless of Allaah's remembrance. When unmindfulness of Allaah's remembrance and the home of the Hereafter is coupled with following of desires, then every evil is

---

[1] Refer to Chapter Thirteen: Ibn al-Qayyim on Making Use of One's Time in Changing Evil into Good.

produced thereby and very frequently one of them is found combined with the other.

(7) Whoever contemplates the corruption of the world, both the general and the specific, will find that it emanates from these two principles.

(8) Heedlessness comes between a servant and his conceiving the truth, becoming acquainted with it and having knowledge of it. Therefore, because of this he becomes of those who are astray (daalleen).

(9) Following of desires prevents him from seeking the truth, desiring it and following it. Therefore he becomes of those with whom Allaah is angry (maghdoobi 'alaihim).

(10) As for those who have been favoured (by Allaah), they are the ones to whom Allaah has been bountiful by granting them the realisation of the truth in terms of knowledge,[2] in complying with it and preferring it as a mode of conduct over whatever is besides it. These are the ones who are upon the path of safety and those besides them are upon the path of destruction.

(11) For this reason Allaah, free from all imperfection, has ordered that we say numerous times, in the day and night:

Guide us upon the Straight Way. The Way of those on whom You have bestowed Your Grace, not (the way) of those who earned Your Anger (such as the Jews), nor of those who went astray (such as the Christians). [Soorah al-Faatihah (1):7].

(12) The servant is in the greatest need of being knowledgeable of what will benefit him in this life and the hereafter, that he prefers and chooses what benefits him and avoids what harms him. By both of these things he is guided to the Straight Way.

(13) If the knowledge of this passes him by he will be treading the path of those who are astray. If his desiring it (i.e., the truth) and

---

[2] Refer to Chapter Two: The Ways of Attaining Knowledge.

following it is lost, he will be treading the path of those upon whom is (Allaah's) anger.

(14) By this (explanation) you will realise the extent and scope of this mighty supplication, the intense need for it and the dependence of the happiness of this life and the hereafter upon it.

THE SERVANT'S EXTREME NEED FOR GUIDANCE

(15) The servant is in need of guidance,[3] at every moment and in every breath, in everything that happens to him and passes him by, for he is in the midst of many matters from which he cannot separate himself:

(i) Matters in which he found himself because of ignorance, rather than guidance, so he is in need of seeking guidance to the truth with respect to these.

(ii) Matters in which he knows the guidance, but did not act upon it in the proper manner, so he is in need of repenting from them.

(iii) There are matters concerning which he did not know the aspect of guidance in them, neither in terms of knowledge nor action. Thus

---

[3] Ibn al-Qayyim said, "Guidance) hidaayah) is:

a)   Elucidation (bayaan) and Indication (dalaalah) (to the path), then

b)   b) Success (tawfeeq) and Inspiration (ilhaarn) (in following the path), and this comes after (the guidance of) elucidation and indication. There is no way to elucidation and indication except by means of the Messengers. So when elucidation, indication and acquaintance (of the path) has been obtained, there will occur, as a result of this the guidance of success (in following the path), the placing of faith (eemaan) in the heart and its beautification and endearment to it, making it (the heart) prefer eemaan, be pleased with it and aspire for it. There are two independent and distinct (types of) guidance. Success and prosperity cannot be gained except by them. They both contain the knowledge and acquaintance of that which we do not know of the truth, in both a general and specific sense, as well as our being inspired to the truth and being made to desire following it inwardly and outwardly. Then (they contain) the creation of the capability for us (by Allaah) to perform the requirements of this guidance with respect to speech, action and firm resolution. (Then after all of this), being made to remain firm and established upon it until death. It is from the above that this extreme need of the servant for making this supplication is above every other need." Madaarijus Saalikeen, p.32.

guidance to both knowledge and acquaintance with them, the desire for them and acting upon them has passed him by.

(iv) There are matters in which he has been guided in one aspect but not in others, so he is in need of perfect and complete guidance with respect to them. Or matters for which he has been guided to their foundations but not -to their particular details, so he is need of a specific guidance (to those particular details).

(v) There are matters to which he has been guided but he is in need of further guidance with respect to them since **guidance to the path** is one thing, but guidance **upon the path** is something else. Do we not see that a man knows the path to a certain city, that the path is such and such. However, he is not capable of traversing this path because traversing it requires specific guidance in the journey itself, such as travelling at a certain time as opposed to another, taking a certain amount of water in such and such a desert, resting at this place as opposed to that one. All of this is guidance upon the journey. The one who (merely) knows that this is the path neglects all of this, perishes and is cut off from the desired goal.[4]

(vi) Likewise there are matters for which he is in need of guidance in the future, similar to (the guidance) that he obtained in the past.

(vii) Matters for which he does not have belief concerning their truthfulness or falsehood and thus he is need of guidance as to what is correct regarding them.

(viii) Matters with respect to which he believes he is upon guidance but, in reality, is upon misguidance and does not realise. He is in

---

[4] The Messenger of Allaah (ρ) said, **"Indeed the Children of Israa'eel split up into seventy-one sects and my Ummah will split up into seventy-three, all of them are in the Fire except one. 'It was said, What is the one?'** He said, **"That which I and my Companions are upon."** Reported by at-Tirmidhee (no. 2792), al-Haakim (1/128~129), al-Laalikaa'ee (no. 147) and others from 'Abdullaah ibn 'Amr ibn al-'Aas (τ). Abul-'Aaliyah (d. 90H) said, **"Allaah has bestowed upon me two favours, I do not know which of them is more superior. That He guided me to Islaam or that He did not make me a Harooree (one of the sects of innovation)."** Reported by al-Laalikaa'ee (no. 230). And Yoosuf ibn Asbaat said, **"My father used to be a Qadaree and my (maternal) uncles used to Raafidees-then Allaah saved me through Sufyaan."** Al-Laalikaa'ee in Sharh Usoolul-I'tiqaad (no. 32).

need of being taken away from that (false) belief by guidance from Allaah.

(xi) Matters which he has acted upon due to guidance so that he is in need of guiding others towards them, directing them and advising them. His neglect of this causes a similar level of (his own) guidance to be lost.

AND MAKE US LEADERS FOR THE PIOUS

(16) When it is known that guiding people, teaching them and advising them opens up a door of guidance for an individual -since the reward for an action is its like - every time he guides someone and teaches him, then Allaah will (further) guide him and teach him. Therefore, he will become a guide and guided, as occurs in the supplication of the Messenger of Allaah (ρ) which has been reported by at-Tirmidhee[5] and others, "O Allaah, beautify us with the adornment of eemaan, make us guides (for others), guided, not astray, leading others astray, peaceful to Your close friends (awliyaa), warring with Your enemies. With Your love do we love those who love You and with Your enmity do we show enmity to those who oppose You."

(17) Allaah, free from all imperfections, praised his believing servants who ask Him to make them leaders who are sought as examples upon guidance. Allaah, the Exalted, said regarding their description:

And those who say, "Our Lord! Bestow on us wives and offspring who will be the comfort of our eyes[6], and make us

---

[5] Its wording in Tuhfatul_Ahwadhee (9/370) is" ,**O Allaah! Make us guides (for others), guided, not astray leading others astray, peaceful to Your close friends (awliyaa), warring with Your enemies. With Your love do we love those who love You and with Your enmity do we show enmity to those who oppose You."** At-Tirmidhee said, "This is a ghareeb hadeeth, we do not know the likes of this from the hadeeth of Ibn Abee Laylaa except from this route." Al-Mubaarakfooree said (9/367) about Ibn Abee Laylaa, "He is Muhammad ibn 'Abdur-Rahmaan Ibn Abee Laylaa al-Ansaaree, al-Koofee, al-Qaadee. He is truthful, but has very poor memory." Shaikh al-Albaanee declared it Da'eeful-Isnaad,' (weak) Da'eef Sunanit-Tirmidhee (678/3659).

[6] At-Tabaree said, 'Upon that which is a comfort to our eyes in that You cause us to see them performing actions of obedience to You.'

an Imaam (leader/guide) for the pious (Muttaqoon)."
[Soorah al-Furqaan (25):74].

(18) Ibn Abbaas said (in explanation of this aayah), "Following our example upon goodness." Aboo Saalih said, "Being guided by our example." Makhool said, "Scholars in (delivering) verdict, the pious guide themselves by our example." Mujaahid said, "Make us follow the example of the pious, guiding ourselves by them."

(19) This explanation (of Mujaahid) has caused difficulty for the one who does not know the greatness of the understanding of the Salaf and the depth of their knowledge and who says, "It is necessary for this aayah with this saying to be turned around, in agreement with the meaning, 'Make the pious (muttaqoon) our leaders.'

(20) Refuge is from Allaah that something should be turned on its face. But this is from the perfect understanding of Mujaahid, for no man can be an Imaam (leader) for the pious until he (himself) follows the example of the pious (in their taqwaa). So Mujaahid made an indication to this aspect (of the meaning) by which they obtain this desired goal (of being leaders) - and that is by seeking the pious (muttaqoon) of the Salaf **before them** as (models of) guidance so that Allaah (in turn) will make them leaders (of guidance) for the pious **after them**. This is the most excellent and most delicate of meanings in the Qur'aan, and it has nothing to do with turning (the meaning) around whatsoever.

(21) So the one who follows the example of the Ahlus-Sunnah who were before him, will be one whose example is followed after him, or by those who are with him.

(22) Allaah, free from all imperfections, made the word 'Imaam' singlular (in the aayah) and did not say, **"And make us leaders (A'immah) for the pious."** Then it is said, 'Imaam in this aayah is the plural of 'aam,' similar to 'sihaab' the plural of 'saahib,' and this is the saying of al-Akhfash, and it is far (from what is correct) and is not from (what is) well-known and famous from the language, such that it should be used to interpret the Qur'aan.

(23) Others have said, 'Imaam' here is a verbal noun, not a proper noun. It is said, 'He led with a leadership,' (amma imaaman), similar to, 'He fasted a fast,' (saama siyaaman) and 'He stood a standing,' (qaama qiyaaman) and so the meaning would be, 'Make us possessors of leadership,'-but this saying is weaker than the previous one.

(24) Al-Farraa' said, "He said, 'As a leader (Imaaman)' and did not say, 'As leaders (A'immatan),' just like in His saying:

Verily, <u>we</u> are a messenger of the Lord of the Worlds. [Soorah Shu'araa (26):16].

He did not say, '**... two messengers of the Lord of the Worlds.'** And this is in the singular by which the plural form is meant, such as in the saying of the poet:

> O my (female) rebukers! Do not increase in censuring me
> Verily, the rebukers are not my leader

meaning, 'they are not my leaders' and this is the best of the sayings save that it is in need of further clarification. That is, the muttaqoon, all of them, are upon a single way, their deity is one, they are followers of one Book, one Prophet and they are the servants of one Lord. Therefore, their religion is one religion, their Prophet is one prophet, their Book is one book and their deity is one deity.

(25) So it is as if they were all a single leader (Imaam) for whoever comes after them. They are not like the opposing leaders (at variance with one another), those whose ways, schools of thought and beliefs are at variance. Therefore, following their example occurs by following what they (the Allaah-fearing from the Salaf) were upon, and that is but a single thing, and that is the leader (Imaam) in reality.[7]

---

[7] i.e., they were all upon one and the same way. So even though they were numerous in number, they are leaders upon one and the same thing and so are like a single (unified) leader upon that way.

LEADERSHIP COMES BY PATIENCE AND CERTAINTY

(26) And He, free from all imperfections, has informed us that this leadership is obtained by patience (sabr) and certainty (yaqeen) for He, the Exalted said:

And We made from among them, leaders, giving guidance under Our Command, when they were patient and believed with certainty in Our Signs. [Soorah as-Sajdah (32):24]

Therefore, it is by patience and certainty that leadership in the religion is obtained.

(27) It is said that it is 'Patience (in keeping) away from the world (by being occupied in worship),' and it is said, 'Patience in the face of trials,' and it is also said, 'Patience in keeping away from the forbidden things.' 'However, what is correct is that leadership is obtained by patience in all of this, patience in fulfilling the obligatory duties of Allaah, patience in avoiding His prohibitions and patience over the decrees (of Allaah).

(28) Allaah put both patience and certainty together since they are both (the source of) the happiness of the servant. Losing them both makes him lose his happiness. The heart is invaded by the various calamities of desires and lusts (shahawaat) which are in opposition to the command of Allaah, and also by the calamities of doubts which are in opposition to His goodness.

(29) Therefore, by patience, the desires and lusts are repelled and with certainty, the doubts are repelled. The desire (shahwah) and the doubt (shubhah) are in opposition to the religion from every single aspect. None will be saved from the punishment of Allaah except the one who repelled his desires with patience and his doubts with his certainty.

(30) This is why Allaah, free from all imperfection, informed about the loss and ruin of the actions of the people of doubts, lusts and desires:

Like those before you, they were mightier than you in power, and more abundant in wealth and children. They had enjoyed their portion awhile, so enjoy your portion awhile as those

before you enjoyed their portion awhile ... [Soorah at-Taubah (9):69].

This enjoyment is their enjoyment of their share of lusts and desires, then He said:

...And you indulged in play and pastime (and in telling lies against Allaah and His Messenger Muhammad) as they indulged in play and pastime... [Soorah at-Taubah (9):69].

And this is arguing with falsehood about the religion of Allaah and it is the argument and fooling around of the people of doubts. Then He said:

...Such are they whose deeds are in vain in this world and in the Hereafter. Such are they who are the losers. [Soorah at-Taubah (9):69].

(31) So Allaah, free from all imperfections, attached the wastage and ruin of ones actions and loss with the following of desires, which is taking enjoyment from one's share of desires, and with the following of doubts, which is arguing by falsehood.

LEADERSHIP IS ALSO BY CALLING TO ALLAAH WITH WHAT HE HAS COMMANDED

(32) Just as He, free from all imperfections, has linked leadership in the religion with patience and certainty, the aayah' also contains two further principles:

(i) The first: Calling to Allaah and to the guidance of His creation.

(ii) The second: Guiding them with what He has commanded, upon the tongue of His Messenger, not what is demanded by their intellects, opinions, political manoeuvres, tastes and the blind-following of their predecessors, without any proof from Allaah. Because He said:

... giving guidance under Our Command, when they were patient ... [Soorah as-Sajdah (32):24].

FOUR PRINCIPLES

(33) So these are the four principles that the aayah contains:

The First Principle: Patience-and that is restraining the soul from the prohibitions of Allaah, keeping it confined to the commandments of Allaah and preventing it from complaining about and becoming angered with His decrees.

The Second Principle: Certainty-and that is firm, established and unshakeable faith in which there is no doubt and (the faith) which does not hesitate, suspect or doubt in the five fundamentals that Allaah, the Exalted, has mentioned in His saying:

It is not Al-Birr (piety, righteousness and obedience to Allaah) that you turn your faces towards east and (or) west (in prayers); but Al-Birr is (the quality of) the one who believes in Allaah, the Last Day, the Angels, the Book and the Prophets. [Soorah al-Baqarah (2):177].

and in His saying:

And whosoever disbelieves in Allaah, His Angels, His Books, His Messengers and the Last Day-then indeed he has strayed far away. [Soorah an-Nisaa (4):136].

and His saying:

The Messenger believes in what has been sent down to him from his Lord, and (so do) the believers. Each one believes in Allaah, His Angels, His Books and His Messengers. They say, 'We make no distinction between one another of His Messengers.' [Soorah al-Baqarah (2):285].

And having faith in the Final Day is included in having faith in the Books and Messengers.

(i) The Messenger (sallallahu alaihiwasallam) combined them all in the hadeeth of Umar in his saying about eemaan, **"That you believe in Allaah, His Angels, His Books, His Messengers and the Final Day."** [reported by al-Bukharee (1/20) and Muslim (1/37) from Umar ibn al-Khattaab]. Whoever does not believe in these five is not a believer.

(ii) Certainty is that a (person's) faith in these fundamentals is strengthened until they become visible to the heart, evident to it, their relationship to keen insight (baseerah) being like the relation of the sun and the moon to the sight (i.e., clearly visible). It is for this reason that one from the Salaf said, "Verily faith (eemaan) is (but) certainty (yaqeen), all of it."

The Third Principle: Guiding the creation and calling them to Allaah and His Messenger ρ. The Exalted said:

And who is better in speech than he who invites (men) to Allaah (Islamic Monotheism), does righteous deeds and says, 'I am one of the Muslims.' [Soorah Fussilat (41):33].

Al-Hasan al-Basree said, "This is the beloved of Allaah, this is the Friend (waliyy) of Allaah. He submitted to Allaah, acted in obedience to Allaah and called the creation to Him."

(i) These types of people are the most-excellent of all the types of people, the highest of them in rank on the Day of Judgement in the Sight of Allaah and those whom Allaah has excluded from the losers (mentioned) in His saying:

By Al-'Asr (the time). Verily man is in loss. Except those who believe, do righteous good deeds, and recommend one another to the truth and recommend one another to patience. [Soorah al-Asr (103):1~3].

(ii) So He, free from all imperfection, swore an oath over the ruin and loss of mankind, but excepted the one who perfected himself with faith and righteous actions and who perfected others by advising them with both of these things (faith and righteous actions). This is why Imaam ash-Shaafi'ee (may Allaah have mercy on him) said, "If all of mankind were to reflect upon Soorah al-Asr, it would suffice them." [8]

(iii) No one can be from among the followers of the Messenger ρ in reality except the one who calls to Allaah with clear insight and evidence (baseerah):

Say (O Muhammad (ρ)), 'This is my way. I invite unto Allaah with keen insight and sure knowledge, I and whosoever follows me.' [Soorah al-Yoosuf (12):10]

(iv) His saying, **"... I invite unto Allaah ..."** explains his way, which he is upon, since his way and the way of his followers is calling to Allaah. Therefore, whoever does not call to Allaah is not upon his way.

(v) And His saying, **"... with keen insight and sure knowledge (baseerah) ..."** (regarding this) Ibn al-A'raabi said, "Al-Baseerah: (meaning) firmness in the religion." And it is said, "Al-Baseerah is

---

[8] Ibn al-Qayyim said, "And an explanation of this is that by the completion and perfection of the four levels, an individual attains the limit in his perfection. The first: Knowing the truth; the second: acting upon it; the third: teaching it to the one who is not conversant with it and the fourth: having patience in learning it, acting upon it and teaching it.

So Allaah, the Exalted, mentioned the four levels in this soorah and He, free from all imperfection, swore an oath in this soorah, by time, that every person is certainly in loss and ruin save those who have faith and do righteous actions. They are the ones who act upon whatever they know of the truth, and this is (yet another level). They recommend each other to the truth. They advise one another by teaching and directing - this is the third level. They recommend each other to patience. They remain patient upon the truth and they advise each other to have patience upon it and to be firm upon it - this is the fourth level.

And this is the limit of perfection, for perfection is that a person should be perfect in his self, as well as one who strives to perfect others. His perfection is achieved by correcting his two strengths, knowledge and action. The correctness of the strength in knowledge is due to faith (eemaan) and the correctness of the strength in action is by righteous actions. His perfecting others is by teaching them, having patience in this and recommending them to have patience upon knowledge and to act upon it. This soorah, despite its brevity, is one of the most comprehensive of the soorahs of the Qur'aan in gathering goodness in its entirety. All praise is due to Allaah who made His Book sufficient (free of need) from everything besides it, a healing for every disease and a guide to every good." Miftaah Daarus-Sa'aadah (1/61).

keen insight, just as it is said to an intelligent person, 'You have baseerah in this,' meaning keen insight. A poet said:

In those who first departed among the generations
Are insights (of sure knowledge) for us

(vi) What is correct is that keen insight is a fruit of sure knowledge. So when one has sure knowledge he has keen and perceptive insight. Whoever lacks sure knowledge lacks insight, and it is as if he has no sure knowledge. The root of this word (baseerah) is from 'dhuhoor' (visibility) and 'bayaan' (elucidation). The Qur'aan consists of basaa'ir (pl. of baseerah), meaning evidences, guidance and elucidation which lead to the truth and guide to right conduct. This is why it is said about the trail of blood which gives evidence to the game animal (that has been shot), that it is 'baseerah.'

(vii) So this aayah indicates that the one who is not upon sure knowledge is not one of the followers of the Messenger ρ whose followers are the ones who possess sure knowledge and keen insights. This is why He said, **"... I and whosoever follows me ..."**

(viii) If the meaning was, "I call upon Allaah, I and whosoever follows me ..." and "... whosoever follows me ..." refers back to the nominative pronoun in "I invite unto ..." and this conjunction has been made for the purpose of clarification, then this is a proof that the followers of the Messenger ρ are the ones who call to Allaah and His Messenger ρ.

(ix) If the wording "... and whosoever follows me ..." is in conjunction with the genitive pronoun in "... my way ..." then the (meaning) is, "This is my way and the way of those who follow me." In both considerations (of the meaning) his ρ path and the path of whoever follows him is calling to Allaah.

The Fourth Principle: (Which is in) His saying:

"... giving guidance under Our Command..." [Soorah as-Sajdah (32):24].

In this is an evidence for the obligation of (their) following what Allaah has revealed to His Messenger ρ and of (their) guidance by it alone, as opposed to the other sayings, opinions, sects and methodologies.[9] Rather, they do not guide (themselves and others) except by His command, specifically.

(34) So from this (it is gathered) that the leaders of the religion who are sought as (models of) guidance, are the ones who have combined patience, certainty and calling to Allaah with the Sunnah and the Revelation, not with opinions and innovations. They are the vicegerents (successors) of the Messenger ρ in his ummah - and they are his special ones and close friends (awliyaa). Whoever shows enmity to them or fights against them has shown enmity to Allaah, the One free of all imperfections, and has waged war against Him.

(35) Imaam Ahmad said in the initial address of his book 'Ar-Radd 'alal-Jahmiyyah,'

"All praise is for Allaah Who, in every age and interval between the Prophets, raises up a group from the People of Knowledge who call the misguided to guidance and patiently bear ill-treatment and harm. With the Book of Allaah they give life to the dead, and by Allaah's light they give sight to the blind. How many a person killed by Iblees have they revived. How many people astray and wandering have they guided. How beautiful their effect has been upon the people, and how vile people have been towards them. They repel from the Book of Allaah the alterations of those going beyond bounds, the false claims of the liars and the false interpretations of the ignorant ones-those who uphold the banner of innovation and let loose the trials and discords. Who differ about the Book, oppose the Book and agree to oppose the Book. Those who speak about Allaah and His Book without knowledge, argue about what is ambiguous in the Book and deceive the ignorant with such ambiguities. We seek refuge in Allaah from the trials of the misguided ones." ['Ar-Radd 'alal-Jahmiyyah waz-Zanaadiqah (p.2) of Imaam Ahmad].

---

[9] Refer to Chapter Eleven: The Methodology of a Muslim.

THE WAYS OF ATTAINING BENEFITS

(36) Amongst the things with which it is desirable to be concerned and occupied in terms of knowledge, acquaintance, intent and desire, is the knowledge that every person - rather every living creature - strives for that which will bring about pleasure, bliss and a good life and which will repel the opposite of that. This is a correct and proper need which comprises six matters:

The first: Knowledge of that which is beneficial to the servant, favourable to him and which will attain pleasure, joy, happiness and a good life for him.

The second: Knowledge of the way which will take him to that.

The third: Traversing upon this way.

The fourth: Knowledge of that which is harmful, injurious and repelling and which makes his life harsh and miserable.

The fifth: Knowledge of the way which, if he adopts, will lead aim to that.

The sixth: Avoiding this way.

(37) So these are six matters and the pleasure of a servant, his joy, happiness and welfare cannot be perfected except by their perfection and any deficiency in them will bring back his bad state and miserable life.

(38) Every intelligent person strives in these matters. However, most people err in attaining this beloved and beneficial need. Either due to lack of knowledge and proper conception or due to not knowing the path which will lead him (to this need). The cause of these two errors is ignorance, and this can be removed with knowledge.

(39) However, sometimes he may have attained knowledge of this need and of the path that will lead him to it, but there are wants and desires in his heart which come between him and his yearning for this beneficial need and traversing its path. Whenever he desires this path, these wants and desires obstruct him and come between him and his desire for this beneficial need.

(40) He will not be able to abandon them (the desires) and give precedence to the beneficial need except by one of two things:

(i) Either **a love that perturbs** (shakes him) or **a fear that discomforts**, (as a result of which) Allaah, His Messenger, the home of the Hereafter, Paradise and its bliss all become more beloved to him than these desires and lusts. He (also) realises that he can never combine both of these things together (in his heart) so he prefers the higher of the two beloved things (to him) over that which is lower.

(ii) Or he attains knowledge of what (unresting) fears and harms he would gather by choosing these lusts and desires, (fears and harms) which are more severe and lasting than the mere pain of missing out on them.

(41) So when these two types of knowledge take root in his heart he will choose what is desirable and will put it ahead of everything that is besides it, **because the special characteristic of intelligence can only be realised by giving preference to the greater of two beloved things over the lesser of the two, and bearing the lesser of two dislikeable/harmful things to escape from the greater of them.**

THE DIVERSITY IN PEOPLES CHOICES AND DECISIONS

(42) By this principle you will know the minds of people and be able to differentiate between the intelligent person and other than him, and the diversity in the (levels of) intelligence of people will become apparent. Where then, is the intelligence of the one who prefers the worldly, exciting (but) troublesome pleasures which are like confused dreams or like an apparition by which he entertains the one who visits him in his dream over the pleasure which is of the greatest of (all) pleasures, and a rejoicing and a delight which is of the greatest of (all) delights, which is everlasting, never ceases, nor perishes and is never cut off? He sells this for a pleasure which fades and perishes, one which is filled with harms and which is only obtained by (undergoing) harms and whose consequences are (but) harms.

(43) If the intelligent person were to compare between the pleasure and harm, pain and benefit of the two, he would become ashamed of himself and of his intelligence. How can he strive to seek it and waste his time by occupying himself with it, let alone preferring it over that which no eye has seen, no ears have heard and has never been conceived of in the heart of man?

(44) Allaah, free from all imperfections, has purchased the souls of the Believers and has made Paradise their price. He put this covenant into effect upon the hand of his Messenger and close friend, the best of His creation. So it is a commodity (i.e., the souls of the Believers) which the Lord of the Heavens and the earth is a purchaser of. The pleasure of looking at His Noble Face and listening to His Speech in His home (of the hereafter) is its price (in return).

(45) How can it befit the intelligent person that he should waste and neglect it, and to sell it for an insignificant price, in a ceasing, wasting, perishing place. Is this but the greatest of frauds? This senseless and foolish fraud will become manifest on the Day of Resurrection, when the scales of those having taqwaa of Allaah will be heavy (with good deeds) and the scales of the falsifiers will be light (devoid of good deeds).

THE PRECURSOR TO THE BLISS OF THE HEREAFTER

(46) When you have known (and understood) this introduction, (then you will realise) that perfect pleasure, rejoicing, happiness, a goodly life and bliss - all of that lies in (having) knowledge of Allaah, in His Tawheed, in being at ease with Him, fondness in meeting with Him and combining one's heart and making one's (sole) concern for Him. For the most troublesome life is the life of the one whose heart is scattered and whose concerns are diverse so that there is no resting place upon which his heart can settle nor any beloved one in whom he can find refuge and comfort. As the poet has explained in his saying:

> (He) does not taste the sweetness of life
> The one for whom there is no beloved
> In which he can find comfort and serenity

(47) A goodly living, a beneficial life and the pleasure of the eye (all) lie in being tranquil and serene with the first (original) beloved (i.e., Allaah) and if the heart were to wander and traverse to all (other) beloved things, it would never be tranquil nor serene. Nor would it find the pleasure of the eye until it was tranquil and serene with its Deity, Lord and Protector, the One besides Whom there is no protector or intercessor. The (heart) does not have any self-sufficiency from Him (even) for the blinking of an eye. As the poet has said:

Take your heart wherever you wish amongst the desires
There is no (real) love except for the first beloved
To how many places in the earth has a youth traversed
(Yet) his everlasting desire is always for the first

(48) Therefore be eager that your concern is only one (concern) and that that is Allaah, alone, because this is the objective of the servant's happiness and the one who is in this condition is in a paradise of this world before the Paradise of the hereafter, and in a present state of bliss. As some of them have said, "Verily, there pass over the heart times about which I say, 'If the people of Paradise are in the likes of these (feelings), then they are certainly in a good life.'" Another one has said, "Verily, there pass over the heart times in which it dances with joy." And another one said, "The paupers of this world depart from it and they do not taste the best of what can be found in it." So it was said, "And what is the best of what can be found in it?" He replied, "Knowing Allaah, loving Him, finding ease and pleasure in nearness to Him and being fond of meeting Him."

(49) There is no pleasure in the world which resembles the pleasure of the People of Paradise with the exception of this one, and for this reason the Prophet ρ said, **"(Two things) from your world have been made beloved to me: women and scent (perfume), and the prayer has been made the pleasure of my eye."**

(50) So he ρ informed that two things from the world have been endeared to him: women and scent and then he said, **"And the prayer has been made the pleasure of my eye."**

(51) "The pleasure of the eye ..." is above (the level of) love, for the eye does not find pleasure with every beloved thing. The eye only finds pleasure in that beloved thing which is loved as (something) in itself, and that is none but Allaah, besides Whom there is none deserving of worship. As for everything that is besides Him, then it is loved (with a love) that follows from His love, so it is loved for His sake and it is not loved along with Him, for loving (something) along with Him is shirk (associationism) and loving (something) for His sake is Tawheed. [Refer to Chapter Three: Ways to Bring About the Love of Allaah].

(52) A pagan takes as equals and rivals others besides Allaah, loving them as only Allaah should be loved. However, the muwahhid (the one who believes in Tawheed) only loves whomever Allaah loves, and he hates whomever Allaah hates. He does whatever he does for the sake of Allaah and he leaves whatever he leaves for the sake of Allaah.

(53) The central core of the religion is based upon these four principles, which are: Love and hate, and resulting from these two are doing and leaving, giving and withholding.

(54) So whoever perfects all of this, so that it is all for Allaah -then such a one has perfected eemaan and whatever is deficient in that which should be for Allaah, then that comes back as a deficiency in the eemaan of the servant.

(55) The intent here is that, that by which the eye finds pleasure is loftier than that which he (merely) loves. The prayer is the pleasure of the eye of those who love, in the life of this world, due to what it contains of secret and intimate conversations with the One besides Whom the eyes do not find pleasure and (besides Whom) the souls do not find tranquillity and serenity, (and what it contains of) comfort and enjoyment by His remembrance, great pleasure on account of submission, nearness to Him - especially in the state of sujood (prostration) - and it is in this state that the servant is the closest to His Lord.

(56) And from this is the saying of the Prophet ρ, **"O Bilaal! Let us find rest and comfort by the prayer."** So know from this, that his ρ comfort and pleasure lies in the prayer, since he has informed that the pleasure of his eye is in the prayer. Where is this compared to the saying of the one who says, "Let us pray and so be at ease from the prayer." [10]

(57) The comfort and rest of the lover and the pleasure of his eye lies in the prayer but the unmindful one who turns away has no share of this. Rather the prayer is too great and burdensome for him. When he stands (for prayer) it is as if he is standing on hot coals, until he finishes from the obligatory section of the prayer. He hastens it and speeds (his performance of it). Thus, there is no pleasure of the eye for him in it and there is no rest and comfort for his heart in it.

(58) Yet the servant, when his eye finds pleasure in something and his heart finds comfort in it, then the hardest thing for him is to separate from it. But the pretender, whose heart is empty of Allaah's remembrance and the home of the hereafter and who is put to trial by the world, the hardest thing for him is the prayer and the most hated thing to him is it's lengthiness, even though he is sound in health, idle and unoccupied.

THE PRAYER OF THE LOVERS[11]

(59) Amongst those things that it is necessary to know is that the prayer by which the eye finds pleasure and by which the heart finds comfort and rest, is the one that combines six matters:

The First-Sincerity of Purpose

(60) And this is that the reason behind the prayer and the thing which calls to it, is the servant's aspiration for Allaah, his love of Him, his seeking His pleasure, nearness to Him, frequently calling upon Him and fulfilling His orders. Such that nothing from the shares of this world constitute a motive for the prayer, ever. Rather, a person comes to the prayer whilst seeking the Face of the Lord, the Most High, out of love for Him, fear of His punishment and hoping for His forgiveness and reward.

---

[10] i.e. let us get the Prayer out of the way so that we can relax.
[11] Refer also to Chapters Four to Ten, related to khushoo (humility and submissiveness) within the prayer.

The Second-Truthfulness and Sincerity of Action

(61) This is when a person vacates his heart for Allaah and strives his utmost in turning himself towards Allaah during the prayer. That within the prayer he gathers his heart together for the prayer and performs it in the best of ways and the most perfect amongst them, both outwardly and inwardly. For the prayer has an outward appearance and an inner one.

(62) Its outward appearance are the observable (physical) actions and motions and the audible sounds. Its inner appearance is humility and submissiveness of the heart (khushoo'), carefully observing oneself, knowing that Allaah is in fact observing the servant (muraaqabah), emptying the heart for Allaah, turning the heart wholly and fully towards Allaah during the prayer and not turning it away from Him to something else. All of these (inner appearances) are like a soul (for the prayer) and the outward actions are like a body (for the prayer). Therefore, when the prayer is lacking a soul, it is like a body without a soul.

(63) Does the servant not feel ashamed then, that he faces his Master with the likes of this? Because of this the prayer is coiled and twisted like the shabby, worn-out garment, and the face of its owner (i.e., performer) is struck with it and it says, "May Allaah waste you as you have wasted me."

(64) The prayer whose outward and inner appearance has been perfected rises (to the heavens) while it has light and manifest proof, just like the light of the sun, until it is brought to Allaah and He is pleased with it and accepts it, and it says, "May Allaah guard you as you have guarded me."[12]

---

[12] Ibn al-Qayyim said in Al-Fawaa'id (p.258), "The servant has two standings in front of Allaah. A standing in front of Him during the prayer and a standing in front of Him on the Day of meeting with Him. Whoever stood for the first standing, giving its due right, the other meeting will become easier for him. And whoever took this standing lightly and did not perform it with its due right, the other standing will become hard and severe for him. The Most High said:

"And during the night, prostrate yourself to Him (i.e., the offering of Maghrib and Ishaa prayers), and glorify Him a long night through (i.e., Tahajjud prayer). Verily!

The Third-Following and Imitating the Messenger and Guiding One's Actions by Him

(65) This is that the servant has great zeal in guiding himself by the Prophet ρ with respect to his prayer, and that he prays as he ρ used to pray whilst turning away and leaving what the people have innovated both with respect to adding and taking away things from the prayer as well as the various fabrications, none of which have been narrated from the Messenger ρ nor from any of the Companions.

(66) Do not give consideration to the sayings of those who make allowances, those who stop and pause (only) at the least of that which they believe to be obligatory even though someone else will have contested with them regarding it, and would have made obligatory that which they have abandoned and dropped. Perhaps the hadeeth are established and the Prophetic Sunnah is right next to them, but they will not turn towards that and will (instead) say, "We are the blind-followers of the madhhab of so and so." [13]

These (disbelievers) love the present life of this world, and put behind them a heavy Day (that will be hard). [Soorah al-Insaan (76):26~27].

[13] Ibn al-Qayyim may Allaah have mercy on him, said in I'Laamul-Muwaqqi'een, (4/177) "Let the muftee beware, the one who fears standing in front of Allaah, free is He from all imperfections, that he answers the questioner with a verdict from his madhhab of which he is a blind-follower, while he knows that in this particular matter, a madhhab other than his own is stronger and is more sound in its evidence. But leadership teaches him to embark boldly in giving a fatwaa with something about which he knows, overwhelmingly, that the truth is in opposition to it. As a result he is a deceitful and dishonest to Allaah, His Messenger and to the questioner. Allaah does not guide the plan of the deceitful and He has forbidden Paradise to the one who meets Him while he has been dishonest to Islaam and its people. And the religion is but giving sincere advice. Dishonesty is an opposite to the religion, just like the opposition of lying to truthfulness and falsehood to truth. And when a matter arises in which we hold an opinion which opposes (our own) madhhab, then we cannot give a verdict in opposition to what we believe (to be correct), therefore we quote the strongest madhhab (in that matter) and give it preference, and we say, 'This is what is correct and it is more deserving of being accepted,' and Allaah grants success." Refer to Chapter Twelve: Ibn al-Qayyim on Following a Madhhab.

Imaam at-Tahaawee may Allaah have mercy on him ,said, "None blindly follows except an ignorant person or a bigoted partisan," reported from him by Ibn 'Aabideen in Rasm al-Muftee (1/32). It is also reported from him by Ibn Hajr al-Asqalaanee in his biography

(67) This is not pure and correct in the sight of Allaah, the Exalted, and it is not an excuse for the one who opposes what he knows from the Sunnah, for Allaah, the Exalted, ordered obedience to His Messenger and following and imitating him alone. He did not command the following of others besides him. Others besides the Messenger ρ are only obeyed when they command only that which the Messenger commanded, and everyone besides the Messenger ρ - his speech can be taken (and accepted) or refused (and rejected).

(68) And Allaah, free is He from all imperfections, the Exalted, has sworn upon His own Noble Self that we do not truly believe until we make the Messenger ρ the sole judge in all disputes that occur between us and until we comply with his judgement and submit to it perfectly and completely. [14]

(69) Referring judgement to someone besides the Messenger ρ will not benefit us and will not deliver us from the punishment of Allaah. The answer (i.e., 'We are the blind followers of the madhhab of so and so ...') will not be accepted from us when we hear His Call, free is He of all imperfection, on the Day of Judgement:

How did you respond to the Messengers? [Soorah Qasas (28):65].

(70) It is definite that He will ask us about that and will request from us an answer. He, the Exalted, said:

---

in Al-Lisaan (1/305), that Aboo 'Ubayd ibn Jurthoomah was revising some questions with him, so he responded to one matter and Aboo 'Ubayd said, "This is not the saying of Aboo Haneefah." So he replied, "O Qaadee! Do I hold everything that Aboo Haneefah said?!" So he said, "I did not think that you were anything but a blind-follower." So he said, "Does anyone blindly follow except a bigoted partisan?" So he said, "Or an ignorant person."

[14] And this due to the saying of Allaah, the Exalted:

But no, by your Lord, they can have no Faith, until they make you (O Muhammad ρ) judge in all disputes between them, and find in themselves no resistance against your decisions, and accept (them) with full submission. [Soorah an-Nisaa (4):65].

Then surely, We shall question those (people) to whom it (the Book) was sent and verily, We shall question the Messengers. [Soorah al-A'raaf (7):6.]

(71) The Prophet ρ said, **"It has been revealed to me that you will be put to trial through me and that you will be questioned about me,"**[15] meaning the questioning in the grave.

(72) Therefore, if the sunnah of the Messenger of Allaah ρ comes to someone and he abandons it for the saying of anyone amongst people, it will be rejected (from him) on the Day of Resurrection and he will come to know (the truth).

The Fourth-Observing Ihsaan

(73) This is (observing) muraaqabah, which is that you worship Allaah as if you are seeing Him. This observance begins with and emanates from perfect faith in Allaah, His Names and His Attributes such that a person sees Allaah, free is He from all imperfection, the Most High, above His heavens, ascending His Throne, speaking with His commands and prohibitions, controlling the affairs of the whole creation, the command coming down from Him and ascending to Him, and actions and the souls (at the point of death) of the servants being presented to Him.

(74) So he witnesses all of that with his hear. He witnesses His Names and His Attributes and he witnesses a Qayyoom (Self-Sustainer and Protector of all that exists), a Hayy (Ever-Living), a Samee' (All-Hearer), a Baseer (All-Seer), an-'Azeez (Mighty), a Hakeem (Most-Wise), one who commands and forbids, loves and hates, there being nothing hidden from Him of the actions of the servants, their statements or their inner condition and realities. Rather, He knows the deception of the eyes and what the hearts conceal.

(75) And this level of Ihsaan is the foundation of all the actions of the heart, for it necessitates veneration and magnification (of

---

[15] Reported by Imaam Ahmad with the wording, "As for the trial of the grave, then by me you will be put to trial and about me will you be questioned." Declared hasan by Shaikh al-Albaanee in Saheehul-Jaami', no. 1361.

29

Allaah), awe and love, repentance and reliance, submission to Allaah, free is He from all imperfection, and humbling oneself to Him. It also cuts off the whisperings and murmurings of the soul and unites the heart and the concern (together) for Allaah.

(76) Therefore, the servant's share of nearness to Allaah is in accordance with his share of observing Ihsaan, and it is with respect to Ihsaan that the prayer (of each individual) differs such that there may be a difference in excellence between the prayer of two men-the difference between their standing, bowing and prostrating being equivalent to the difference between the heavens and the earth.

The Fifth-Seeing that the Blessing is from Allaah

(77) This is that a person witnesses that the favour and blessing belongs to Allaah, free is He from all imperfections, in that He made the person and his family stand in this position, and He also granted them successes in making their hearts and bodies stand in service to Him. Therefore, if it had not been for Allaah, free is He from all imperfections, nothing of this would have occurred. As the Companions used to say, whilst in front of the Prophet ρ:

> By Allaah, if it had not been for Allaah
> We would not have found guidance
> And we would not have given charity
> And nor would we have prayed

(78) Allaah, the Exalted, said:

They regard as a favour upon you (O Muhammad (ρ)) that they have embraced Islaam. Say, "Count not your Islaam as a favour upon me. Nay, but Allaah has conferred a favour upon you, that He has guided you to the Faith, if you indeed are true." [Soorah al-Hujuraat (49):17].

For Allaah, free is He from all imperfections, is the One who made a Muslim a Muslim and the one who prays to be one who prays, as al-Khaleel (i.e., Ibraaheem) said:

"Our Lord! And make us Muslims (submissive unto You) and of our offspring a Muslim nation (submissive unto You), and show us our Manaasik (all the ceremonies of pilgrimage, Hajj and 'Umrah, etc.,)..." [Soorah al-Baqarah (2):128].

(79) And he said:

"O my Lord! Make me one who performs Salaah and (also) from my offspring..." [Soorah Ibraaheem (14):40].

So (granting) the blessing and favour belongs to Allaah alone in that He made His servant to be obedient to Him. This is of the greatest of His blessings over him, and the Exalted said:

"And whatever of blessings and good things you have, it is from Allaah." [Soorah an-Nahl (16):53].

(80) And He said:

But Allaah has endeared the faith to you and has beautified it in your hearts, and has made disbelief, wickedness and disobedience (to Allaah and His Messenger (ρ)) hateful to you. These! They are the rightly guided ones. (This is) a Grace from Allaah and His Favour. And Allaah is All-Knowing, All-Wise. [Soorah al-Hujuraat (49):7~8].

This matter (seeing that the blessing is from Allaah) is one of the greatest of observances and the most beneficial of them for the servant. Every time the servant is greater and stronger in his tawheed, his share of this observance is more perfect and complete.

(81) It has a number of benefits: That it comes in between the heart and becoming amazed with the action and looking at it (with admiration). When a person sees that it is Allaah who favoured him with it, who granted him success in performing it and who guided him to it, this will keep him from looking at his own self, becoming amazed with his action and assailing the people (with this action he did). So he removes this from his heart and does not become amazed with it, and (he removes it) from his tongue and does not show it (to others) and nor does he start demanding things for it. This is the sign of an action that is raised (to Allaah).

(82) And amongst its benefits is that he attributes the praise to the One who deserves it and its (true) owner. He does not see any praise for himself, but in fact he witnesses it, all of it, for Allaah, just as he witnesses that the blessing and favour is all from Allaah. That the bounty is all from Allaah, and that all goodness is in His Hand. This is from the completion of Tawheed.

(83) His heart will not be established upon Tawheed except with this knowledge and witnessing of this knowledge. When he knows this and it becomes firmly rooted in him, it will become a marvel to him and when it becomes a marvel to his heart, it will produce for him - from (the fruits of) love and intimacy with Allaah, fondness of meeting Him, enjoying His remembrance and obeying Him - that for which there is no comparison in the greatest pleasure of the world, ever.

(84) There is no goodness for any man in his life when his heart is hindered from this and when the path towards it is obstructed, but he is as Allaah, the Exalted, has said:

Leave them to eat and enjoy, and let them be preoccupied with (false) hope. Soon will they will come to know!   [Soorah al-Hijr (15):3]

The Sixth-Seeing Deficiency in Oneself

(85) This is that even when the servant strives his utmost in fulfilling an order and sacrifices (himself) in abundance, he is still negligent and the right of Allaah over him is much greater (than his striving). That which should be given (to Him) of obedience and servitude is many times more than that. His Might and Grandeur, free is He from all imperfections, requires such servitude that is necessitated by these two (qualities of Him).

(86) When the aides of the kings and their servants serve in obedience to them whilst honouring them, aggrandizing them, showing them respect and reverence, displaying modesty, having fear and awe of them and being sincere (in advice to them) - such that they empty their hearts and single out their limbs for (service) to these kings - then the King of all kings, the Lord of the Heavens and the Earth is more deserving of being served with multiples of (all of) that.

(87) So when the servant sees in himself that he has not given to His Lord, with regard to His servitude, His due right, not even close to His due right, he will come to know of his negligence and shortcoming and failure to fulfil that which is fitting for Allaah, from His due right (upon His servant), and that he is in greater need of Allaah's forgiveness and His pardon (with respect to the shortcoming in servitude to Him) than that he should request reward from Him for his servitude.

(88) If he had fulfilled his servitude (to Allaah) truly and properly, that would have been as was due of him because of the requirement of servitude ('uboodiyyah) to Allaah. For the servant's serving of his master is a duty upon him because he is his servant and subject. So if he were to request some recompense for his actions and his service (to his master), the people would consider him foolish, stupid. Yet this is when he is not in reality his (master's) servant and subject. In reality, he is the servant of Allaah and His subject, from every single aspect. Therefore, his work and his service is a right due from him because he is His servant. If Allaah were to reward him for that, then that would be a mere blessing, favour and benevolence towards the servant, which he does not deserve.

(89) It is from this (perspective) that the Messenger ρ said, **"None of you shall enter Paradise on account of his actions (alone)." It was said, "Not even you, O Messenger of Allaah?" He replied, "Not even me, unless Allaah covers me with His mercy."** [16]

(90) And Anas ibn Maalik said, "Three scrolls will be brought out for the servant on the Day of Judgement. A scroll of his good deeds, a scroll for his evil deeds and a scroll containing the favours and blessings that Allaah bestowed upon him. The Lord, free from all imperfections, will say to His favours and blessings, 'Take your due right from the good deeds of My servant.' He will say to the smallest

---

[16] Reported by Bukhaaree (7/ 157) and Muslim (4/2170) with his wording, **"None of you will have his actions enter him into Paradise." They said, "Not even you, O Messenger of Allaah?" He said, "Not even me, unless Allaah covers me with blessing and mercy."**

favour (ever bestowed upon him), 'Take your due right from the good deeds of My servant.' So the smallest favour will stand (to take its due right) but the good deeds of the servant will be exhausted. Then (this smallest favour) will say, 'By your Might-my due right has not been fulfilled.' Then when Allaah wishes to show mercy to His servant, He bestows blessings upon him, forgives his sins and multiplies his good deeds."

(91) This is amongst the clearest of evidences of the perfect knowledge of the Companions concerning their Lord and His rights over them, just as they are the most knowledgeable of the ummah concerning the Prophet ρ, his compassion and his Religion. There is contained in this narration such knowledge and cognisance which none but those of keen insight and those having knowledge of Allaah's Names, Attributes and His due right, can grasp.

(92) It is from this that the saying of the Prophet ρ can be understood, in the hadeeth which is reported by Aboo Daawood and Imaam Ahmad, from the hadeeth of Zaid bin Thaabit and Hudhaifah ibn al-Yaamaan and others, that, "If Allaah were to punish the inhabitants of His Heavens and the inhabitants of His Earth, then He would certainly punish them and this would entail no injustice on His part (ever). And if He was to show them mercy, then His Mercy would be better for them than their own actions." [17]

CONCLUSION

(93) And (finally), the chief and fundamental issues of this whole affair are four:

(i)   a correct intention
(ii)   overwhelming strength which is accompanied by (both)
(iii)   aspiration (raghbah) and
(iv)   awe (rahbah)

---

[17] He said in 'Awnul-Ma'bood, "And in its chain of narration is Aboo Sinaan ash-Shaybaanee whom Yahyaa ibn Ma'een and others declared trustworthy and Imaam Ahmad and others spoke about him." (12/467). This hadeeth is declared authentic by Shaikh al-Albaanee in Saheeh Sunan Abee Daawood, no. 3932 and researched in Zilaalul-Jannah (no. 245).

(94) These four matters are the principles in this whole affair and whenever any deficiency occurs in a servant, in his eemaan, in his condition, his inner-self and his outward appearance, then that is due to the deficiency in these four matters, or in some of them.

(95) Therefore, let the wise person contemplate over these four things and let him make them (as the road upon which he) travels and traverses. (And let him) construct (all of) his knowledge, actions, sayings and states (of being) upon them. No one who progresses does so except by them and no one who falls behind does so except by losing them.

(96) Allaah is the One from whom aid is sought, upon Him is the placing of trust and to Him is (one's) longing and hope. He is the One requested to grant us and all of our brothers from Ahlus-Sunnah success in actualising these four principles, in knowledge and action, indeed He is capable of that and the One who bestows it. Sufficient is He for us and He is the best disposer of affairs.

(97) The treatise has been completed by the blessing of Allaah and His praise, there is no partner to Him. The dominion belongs to Him as does the praise and He has power over all things. May Allaah send prayers and many salutations upon our chief, Muhammad, the unlettered Prophet, and upon his family and his Companions, till the Day of Judgement.

Aameen, aameen.

Chapter One

THE SOUND HEART

Ibn al-Qayyim (may Allaah have mercy on him) said, "And the sound heart is the one which is secure from shirk, hatred, jealousy, envy, covetousness, pride, love of the world and leadership. So it is safe from every harmful thing which distances it from Allaah and it is safe from every doubt that contradicts His information (i.e., Revelation). It is safe from every desire that opposes His command and from every wish that competes (repels) what He intends (from His servants), and it is also safe from everything that cuts it off from Allaah. So this sound and safe heart is in a paradise in this world and in a paradise in the barzakh and in a paradise on the Day of Resurrection. The heart's safety and soundness cannot be perfected, absolutely, until it is secure from five things:

(i)   From shirk which nullifies tawheed
(ii)   From innovation which opposes the Sunnah
(iii)   From a desire/lust that opposes the command (of Allaah)
(iv)   From heedlessness that contradicts remembrance (of Him)
(v)   From a desire that nullifies purity and sincerity (in intent and purpose)

These five are barriers to Allaah and beneath each of them are many other categories that contain unique issues which cannot be enumerated. [al-Jawaab al-Kaafee (1/176)].

Chapter Two

THE WAYS OF ATTAINING KNOWLEDGE[18]

And the beneficial knowledge has certain ways and means by which it is obtained and certain paths that are taken in its acquisition and memorisation. Amongst the most important of them are:

Firstly: That the servant asks his Lord for the beneficial knowledge and that he seeks assistance by Him, the Exalted, and shows his need to Him. Allaah ordered His Prophet, Muhammad (ρ) to ask Him that He increases him in knowledge, in addition to his knowledge. He, the Exalted said:

And say, "O Lord! Increase me in knowledge." [Soorah Taa Haa (21):114].

And the Messenger (ρ) used to say, **"O Allaah, benefit me with what you have taught me and teach me that which will benefit me and increase me in knowledge."** [Reported by at_ Tirmidhee (5/578) and Ibn Maajah (1/92). Also refer to Saheeh Ibn Maajah (1/47)].

Secondly: And this is the greatest and the essence of them all - sincerity in seeking the knowledge. The Messenger (ρ) said, **"Whoever learnt knowledge by which the Face of Allaah is to be sought, but does not do so except for attaining a goal of this world, (he) will not smell the fragrance of Paradise on the Day of Resurrection."** [Reported by Aboo Daawood with his wording in Kitaabul-Ilm and Ibn Maajah in his introduction (1/93). Refer also to Saheeh Ibn Maajah (1/48)].

Thirdly: Striving and exerting oneself in seeking knowledge, having keen interest for it, having a true desire in which the Pleasure of Allaah, the Most High, is sought and adopting all of the ways and means in seeking knowledge of the Book and the Sunnah.[19]

---

[18] From AL-Hikmah fid-Da'wah Ilallaah, (pp. 50~53) of Sa'eed ibn 'Alee ibn Wahf al-Qahtaanee, with modifications and additions.

[19] Such as buying books and cassettes, connecting with the people of knowledge from Ahlus-Sunnah, not Ahlul-Bid'ah, attending their gatherings, talks and conferences,

A man came to Aboo Hurairah (τ) and said, "I desire to learn the knowledge but I fear that I may waste it." So Aboo Hurairah replied to him, "Your abandonment of learning it is sufficient in wasting it." [Refer to Tafseerus-Sa'dee (5/194)].

For this reason one of the wise people, upon being asked, "What is the way by which knowledge is obtained?" answered, "With eagerness is it followed, with love is it listened to, with sole concern is it gathered, teach your knowledge to the one who is ignorant, and learn from the one who teaches, for if you do that, you will come to know that of which you were ignorant and you will memorise that which you (yourself) have learnt." [Jaami Bayaanul-Ilm wa Fadlihi of Ibn Abdul-Barr (1/102,103)].

For this reason, Imaam ash—Shaafi'ee (may Allaah have mercy on him) said:

"My brother! You will not acquire knowledge
except by six matters,
I will inform you of their detail with an explanation:
Intelligence, zeal, striving, competence/proficiency
The companionship of a teacher ...
and a long time!"

Fourthly: Avoiding all disobedience by having taqwaa of Allaah, the Most High, for that is the greatest of means of acquiring knowledge, as He, the Most High, has said:

Have taqwaa of Allaah and Allaah will teach you, and Allaah has knowledge of every single thing. [Soorah al-Baqarah (2):282].

And He, the Most High, also said:

O you who believe! If you have taqwaa of Allaah, He will grant you a criterion (to judge between truth and falsehood). [Soorah al-Anfaal (8):29].

---

travelling for the sake of knowledge and other such efforts. Refer to Chapter Eleven: The Methodology of a Muslim.

This is clear and manifest proof that the one who has taqwaa of Allaah, He will grant him knowledge by which he will distinguish between truth and falsehood. For this reason Abdullaah ibn Mas'ood (τ) said, "Indeed, I consider that a man loses knowledge which he once had, due to a sin which he committed." [Jaami' Bayaanul-'ILm wa Fadlihi of Ibn 'Abdul-Barr (1/196)].

Imaam ash_Shaafi'ee (may Allaah have mercy on him) said, "I complained to Wakee' about the poorness of my memory. So he directed me to abandon disobedience. And informed me that the knowledge of Allaah is light. And that the light of Allaah is not given to the disobedient." [Deewaanush-Shaafi'ee (p.88). Refer also to Al-Jawaab al-Kaafee of Ibn al-Qayyim (p.104).]

Imaam Maalik said to Imaam ash-Shaafi'ee (may Allaah have mercy on them both), "I see that Allaah has placed light in your heart so do not extinguish it with the darkness of disobedience." [Al-Jawaab al-Kaafee of Ibn al-Qayyim (p.104)].

Fifthly: Being neither shy nor arrogant in seeking knowledge, and this is why 'Aa'ishah, (may Allaah be pleased with her), said, "How excellent are the women of the Ansaar, shyness/modesty does not prevent them from understanding the religion." [Reported by Bukhaaree in Kitaabul-Ilm].

Umm Sulaim, (may Allaah be pleased with her), said, "O Messenger of Allaah! Allaah is not ashamed of the truth, so is it necessary for a women to make ghusl when she has a wet dream?" The Prophet (ρ) said, **"If she sees the fluid."** [Reported by Bukhaaree in Kitaabul-Ilm].

Mujaahid said, "The shy person and the arrogant one will not learn the knowledge." [Reported by Bukhaaree in Kitaabul-Ilm].

And finally: Acting upon the knowledge. The Messenger of Allaah (ρ) said, **"A servants two feet will not move on the Day of Judgement until he is questioned about four (things). His youth-how he spent it; his knowledge-how he acted upon it; his wealth-how he earned it and how he spent it and his body-how he used/wasted it."** [Reported by at-Tirmidhee (2417) and see Saheehut-Targheeb wat-Tarheeb (1/126)].

He (ρ) also said, **"A man will be brought on the Day of Judgement and will be thrown into the Fire and his entrails will pour out. It will be said, Did you not used to order the good and forbid the evil?' He will say, 'I used to command you with good and not do it myself and I used to forbid you from evil and do it myself."** [Reported by Bukhaaree (3094) and Muslim (2989).

Chapter Three

WAYS TO BRING ABOUT THE LOVE OF ALLAAH

Ibn al-Qayyim (may Allaah have mercy on him) said, "Chapter: Ways that bring about the Love (of Allaah) and necessitate it, and they are ten in number.

One: Recitation of the Qur'aan with reflection and understanding of its meanings and what is intended by it, as one reflects over a book which he has memorised and which he expounds so that he may understand what its author intends from him.

Two: Getting closer to Allaah with the supererogatory acts of worship, after the obligatory ones, for they will take him to another level of love that comes after love.

Three: Constant remembrance in every circumstance by the tongue, the heart, actions and (one's) condition [20], so a person's share of love is in accordance with his share of this remembrance.

---

[20] All of that being based upon what conforms to and is restricted by the Messenger's Sunnah and not upon what the astray Soofees invent and innovate of misguidances and corrupt practices from their own intellects, satanic whisperings and innovatory ejaculations of the mind and soul.

Ibn al-Qayyim said, "He (i.e., Shaikhul-Islam Ibn Taymiyyah) said, 'And as for what many of the people of imaginations and foolishness say, 'Haddathanee qalbee 'an Rabbee' (meaning) 'My heart informed me from my Lord-,then it is correct that his heart informed him. However from whom? His devil or from His Lord? When he says, 'My heart informed me from my Lord,' he is ascribing this informing to someone about whom he does not know whether such a one actually informed him or not. And this is a lie. And the muhaddath of this Ummah [(i.e., 'Umar ibn al-Khatatab) in reference to the hadeeth in Bukhaaree, "Indeed, in the nations before you there were people who were inspired (muhaddathoon) and if there was one in this Nation it would be 'Umar ibn al-Khattaab,"] never used to say this and this saying (i.e., 'My heart informed me from my Lord...') was never uttered by him on a single day. Allaah protected him from saying that. In fact his scribe wrote one day, 'This is what Allaah showed to the Chief of the Believers, 'Umar ibn al-Khattaab.' So he (Umar) said, "No. Erase it and write, 'This is what Umar ibn al-Khattaab saw. If it is correct it is from Allaah and if it is wrong then it is from 'Umar, and Allaah and His Messenger are free from it.' And he said, 'I speak about it with my opinion. If it is correct it is from Allaah and if it is wrong it is from me and Shaytaan.' So this is the saying of al-Muhaddath (i.e., Umar) who has the testification of the Messenger (r) and you will see the one believing in the Divine Union

Four: Preferring His love over your own when desires overcome you and climbing to reach His love, even if the ascent is difficult.

Five: The heart's comprehension of His Names and Attributes, witnessing them and having knowledge of them, to immerse himself in the garden of this knowledge and its fundamental pillars.[21] Whoever knows Allaah by His Names, Attributes and Actions, will, no doubt, love Him. For this reason the deniers of His Attributes (Mu'attilah), Fir'awniyyah and Jahmiyyah are like highway robbers to the hearts, (they come in between it and) between reaching the beloved (i.e., Allaah).[22]

---

with Allaah (Ittihaadee) and the one believing in the inclusion of Allaah in His creation or parts of His creation (Huloolee) and the licentious unrestrained strayer giving rise to forgery saying, 'My heart has informed me from My Lord.'

So look at these two sayings (that of 'Umar and that of those claiming to receive knowledge of Allaah directly, from their hearts) and (look at) these two grades, those who say both these sayings (i.e., 'Umar and those making this claim) and these two states (that of 'Umar and of those besides him) and give every owner of a right his due right and do not make the counterfeit/impostor and the sincere, one and the same thing." Madaarijus-Saalikeen (1/64).

[21] Imaam at-Tirmidhee (d.279H) said, "It has been stated by more than one person from the People of Knowledge about such ahaadeeth, that there is no resemblance (tashbeeh) to the Attributes of Allaah, and our Lord, the Blessed and Most High, descends to the lowest heaven every night. So they say, 'Affirm these narrations, have faith in them, do not deny them, nor ask how.' The likes of this has been related from Maalik ibn Anas, Sufyaan ath-Thawree, Ibn 'Uyainah and 'Abdullaah ibn al-Mubaarak, who all said about such ahaadeeth, 'Leave them as they are, without asking how.' Such is the saying of the People of Knowledge from the Ahlus-Sunnah wal-Jamaa'ah. However, the Jahmiyyah oppose these narrations and say, 'This is resemblance (tashbeeh)!' However, Allaah the Most High, has mentioned in various places in His Book, the Attribute of Hand, Hearing and Seeing, but the Jahmiyyah interpret (make ta'weel) of these aayaat, explaining them in a way other than how they are explained by the People of Knowledge. They say, 'Indeed, Allaah did not create Aadam with His own Hand,' they say that Hand means the Power of Allaah." Sunan at-Tirmidhee (3/24).

[22] Al-Haafidh Taqiyud-Deen Aboo Muhammad 'Abdul-Ghaniyy al-Maqdisee (d.600H) (may Allaah have mercy on him) said, "And know, may Allaah have mercy upon you, that Islaam and its people are attacked and destroyed by three groupings.

(i)   A group who reject the hadeeth pertaining to the Attributes of Allaah and who reject their narrators. They are more harmful to Islaam and its adherents than the Disbelievers.

44

Six: Witnessing His generosity, His benevolence, His favours and blessings, both hidden and open, for these things call to His love.

Seven: And this is the most amazing of them all, the heart's total defeat and humility in front of Allaah, the Most High, and there are no other words and considerations which give expression to this meaning.

Eight: Being alone at the Time of the Descent of Allaah[23] for having private conversations with Him, reciting His Words, investigating the heart, displaying the manners of servitude whilst in front of Him and then to seal all of that with seeking forgiveness and repentance.

Nine: Sitting with the truthful lovers (of Allaah) and gathering the good fruits (arising) from their speech, just as one picks out the best of fruits, and that you do not speak except when the benefit of the speech prevails and when you know that there is a betterment for you and benefit for others in it.

Ten: Keeping distant from everything that comes between the heart and between Allaah, the Mighty and Majestic.

So from these ten ways, the lovers will reach the (various) levels of love and will enter upon the Beloved. And the chief and fundamental principle behind all of this comprises two matters: preparing the soul for this matter and opening the eye of keen insight/sure knowledge." [Madaarijus-Saalikeen (3/17).

Chapter Four

THE PRAYER AND ITS EFFECT UPON ABANDONING SINS AND DEVELOPING THE SOUL[24]

Allaah, the Sublime said:

Indeed prayer restrains from the obscene and evil deeds.
Soorah al-Ankaboot [(29:45)].

Allaah has explained in this aayah that a correct prayer, performed with humility and submissiveness (khushoo') undoubtedly prevents its performer from obscene and evil deeds and leads him to goodness. Therefore, you will see that the people of the mosque are the most superior of mankind and the best amongst them. The sins and shortcomings of others are many times more than the sins and shortcomings of these people.

If the prayer does not prevent us from obscene and evil deeds then it is necessary to carefully scrutinise the deficiency within it and to correct it. There is no escaping from correcting one's prayer and there is no fleeing from bringing about khushoo' within it. So let us look at the causes and let us strive to treat them with the cure, just as we treat our bodies for their diseases. However the treatment of the souls is more appropriate and comes first, and this is what will help us to understand the saying of the Messenger (ρ), **"The first thing for which a servant will be held to account is his prayer. If it is correct and sound, all the rest of his actions will be correct and sound, and if it is corrupt then all the rest of his actions will be corrupt."** [Reported by at-Tabaraanee in Al-Awsat and Ad-Diyaa from Anas (τ). It is also in Saheehul-Jaami no. 2570].

So in the correction of the prayer lies the correction of all the other actions. The position of the prayer (relative to all the other actions) is like that of the head to the body. This is because the servant is

---

[24] From As-Salaat wa Atharuhaa fee Ziyaadatil-Eemaan wa Tahdheebin-Nafs, of Husain al-Awaa'ishah, with slight additions and modification.

nearest to his Lord during his prayer. He calls upon his Lord and seeks forgiveness from Him. He returns to Allaah and cries to Him, the Sublime.

The prayer cannot be corrected except with the correction of the creed, being observant of Allaah, having fear of Him, bringing oneself to account in front of Him, and trembling out of fear of His Fire. When he finishes his prayer and is put to trial with sins and disobedience, he finds strength in his heart to repel them. This is because he looks at the temporary and vanishing pleasures and then at the bliss and joy which never ends and the happiness which is never cut off. So he puts the good which will remain (and last forever) ahead of that which is only transitory and vanishes.

The prayer of the servant is corrupted due to lack of the careful observance of Allaah and weakness in taqwaa.[25] A person is, therefore, not able to produce such awe as will come between him and his acts of disobedience.

There also occurs in the hadeeth, **"Indeed, there is in the body a morsel of flesh, if it is sound and wholesome, then the whole body will be sound and wholesome and if it is corrupt, the whole body will be corrupt. Indeed it is the heart."** [Reported by Bukhaaree, Muslim and others from an-Nu'maan ibn Basheer (τ)].

In the correction and purification of the heart lies the correction of the whole body and in the corruption of the heart lies the corruption of the whole body. If the heart is corrected, the hand will be corrected so that it does not steal or strike anyone or commit zina by touching what is unlawful. The feet will also be corrected so that they do not walk towards what is unlawful. The ears will be put straight so that they do not listen to musical instruments, slander or backbiting. The situation of the tongue will improve so that it does not speak except what is good. If the heart is corrupted, the whole

---

[25] The taabi'ee, Talq ibn Habeeb was asked to define taqwaa. He said, "Taqwaa is to act in obedience to Allaah, hoping for His Mercy upon a light from Him. And taqwaa is to abandon acts of disobedience to Allaah, out of fear of Him upon a light from Him." Reported by Ibn Abee Shaibah in his Kitaabul-Eemaan, no. 99. Ibn al-Qayyim (may Allaah have mercy on him) explained the phrase, "... upon a light from Him ..." to mean pure and correct faith, that nothing but pure faith initiated the servant to perform the action. [Transl. note]

body becomes corrupt and the limbs will not depart except towards evil conduct and mischief.

The matter of the heart is either set aright or corrupted by the prayer. If the prayer is good it is an indication that the heart has benefited and that it is sound and wholesome. If it is not good, it is an indication of the heart receiving little benefit and of its corruption. Evil deeds then become manifest and overtake the limbs.

Know that every prayer which is performed with awe and humility enlivens the heart and stimulates it to do good deeds and also makes it adapt to good deeds, just as every good action which is performed outside of the prayer increases ones khushoo' within the prayer. In a hadeeth there occurs, **"Upon you is the Night Prayer (Tahajjud) as it was the habit of the righteous people before you. It is a means of nearness to Allaah, the Exalted, a prevention from evil deeds and an expiation for sins."** [Reported by Ahmad in his Musnad, at-Tirmidhee and others. It is also in Saheehul-Jaami, no. 3957].

The Messenger (ρ) has made it clear that the Night Prayer is a prevention from sins in that it stops the one who performs it from evil deeds and incites him to do good deeds. Therefore, it is necessary for us to establish the prayer and to increase in it. Likewise we must perform the Night Prayer, standing awestruck, humble and submissive to Allaah, the Sublime, our hearts weeping over what we have neglected and fallen short of while hoping for the mercy of our Lord. We seek nearness to him by calling Him by His Names and Attributes, asking Him by them that he establishes us (upon His path) and that He gives us benefit from our prayer and standing at night.

It was said to the Prophet (ρ), "So and so prays the whole of the night, yet when he reaches the morning he steals!" He (ρ) said, **"What you say (i.e., about his prayer) should prevent him from that..."** or he said, **"His prayer will prevent him (from that)."**[26]

---

[26] Reported by Ahmad, Bazzaar and others. Shaikh al-Albaanee declared it authentic in Silsilatul-Aahaadeeth ad-Da'eefah, vol.1, p.16, in relation to the false hadeeth,

When the prayer of the servant reaches its goal in preventing him from sin and disobedience it is written for him in Iliyyeen as is mentioned in the hadeeth, **"If a prayer is performed after another prayer and there is no foolishness (vain talk) between them, it is written in Illiyyeen."** [Reported by Aboo Daawood and others. It is also in Saheehul-Jaami, no.3731].

Therefore, the performance of prayer with earnestness and bringing together the elements of love, fear, hope, awe and reverence, all of which are constituents of khushoo' is a necessary and vital matter. As is well known, the difference between an accepted prayer and a rejected one is khushoo'. Ibn al-Qayyim mentions in Al-Madaarij, "Two people pray in the same row, behind the same Imaam-and the difference between the prayers of the two is like the distance between the heavens and the earth." And this is because in one heart is khushoo' and in the other heart-which is dead and has found more pleasure in escaping to the valleys of the world-there is the darkness of heedlessness.

"Whoever is not prevented by his prayer from committing obscene and evil deeds does not increase except in distance from Allaah."

Chapter Five

IBN AL-QAYYIM ON THE HADEETH QUDSEE
"I have Divided the Prayer Between Myself and My Servant"

Aboo Hurairah (τ) said, "I heard the Prophet (ρ) say, '**Allaah, the Mighty and Sublime, has said: I have divided the prayer between Myself and My servant into two halves. And My servant shall have what he has asked for. When the servant says:**

All praise belongs to Allaah the Lord of all Creation.
Allaah, the Mighty and Majestic, says, "My servant has praised Me."
And when he says:

The Most Gracious, the Most Merciful.
Allaah, the Mighty and Majestic, says, "My servant has extolled Me."
And when he says:

Master of the Day of Judgement.
Allaah, the Mighty and Majestic, says, "My servant has glorified Me..." and on one occasion He said, "My servant has submitted to My power." And when he says:

You alone do we worship and from You alone do we seek help.
He says, "This is between Me and My servant, and My servant shall have what he has asked for." And when he says:

Guide us to the Straight Path, the Path of those whom You have favoured, not of those upon whom is Your anger, nor of those who are astray.
He says, "This is for My servant, and My servant shall have what he has asked for.'" [27]

---

[27] Reported by Muslim, Maalik, at-Tirmidhee, Aboo Daawood, an-Nasaa'ee and Ibn Maajah.

Ibn al_Qayyim (may Allaah have mercy on him) said, "And when he says, All praise is due to Allaah, the Lord of all Creation ..." he pauses for a short while waiting for the response of his Lord, **"My servant has praised Me."** Then when he says, "The Most Merciful, the Bestower of Mercy"...he waits for the response, **"My servant has extolled Me."** And when he says, "Master of the Day of judgement..." he waits for the response, **"My servant has glorified Me."**

It is the delight of his heart, the pleasure of his eye and the joy of his soul that his Lord says about him, **"My servant..."** three times. By Allaah! If the fumes of desire-and the darknesses of the soul were not upon the hearts, they would have flown out of happiness and joy that their Lord, Maker and Deity says, **"My servant has praised Me, My servant has extolled Me and My servant has glorified Me."**

Then there would have been space in his heart to witness (the reality) of the three names which are the basis of all the Beautiful Names and these are: Allaah, ar-Rabb and ar-Rahmaan.

When he says, "Master of the Day of judgement..." he witnesses the glory which befits none but the King, the Truth, the Manifest. So he witnesses a very powerful and compelling King, to Whom the whole creation has yielded, to Whom the faces are humbled, to Whom the creation humbles itself, and to Whom every possessor of power and honour submits. He witnesses with his heart a King (Who is) upon the Throne of the Heaven.

And then he says, "You alone do we worship and from You alone do we seek help..." in which lies the secret of the creation and the affair of the world and the hereafter, and which contains the loftiest of goals and the most excellent of means (of approach to Allaah). The loftiest of goals is enslavement to Allaah and the most excellent of means is His help and assistance. There is no deity deserving of worship in truth except Him and there is no helper in His worship besides Him. Therefore, His worship is the greatest of goals and His aid is the loftiest of means.

And these words contain the two types of tawheed and they are Tawheed ar-Ruboobiyyah and Tawheed al-Uloohiyyah. Devotion to Allaah comprises His names ar-Rabb and Allaah, so He is worshipped on account of His Uloohiyyah,[28] help is sought from Him on account of His Ruboobiyyah[29] and He guides to the Straight Path on account of His Mercy. The first part of the soorah (i.e., Soorah al-Faatihah) therefore, mentions His names Allaah, ar-Rabb and ar-Rahmaan for the purpose of the one who seeks His worship, help and guidance. He is alone in being able to bestow all of that. There is no one who can aid others in Allaah's worship besides Allaah and none can guide (to the Straight Path) except Him.

---

[28] Uloohiyyah: A term denoting that Allaah is the only One to Whom all forms of worship should be directed in truth, whether actions of the heart (feelings), words and statements or actions of the limbs. The word Ilaah is derived from it, meaning: something that is adored, worshipped, turned to i.e., an object of worship, subservience and adoration. There is nothing else besides Him who deserves that, and this is the meaning of the testimony, 'Laa ilaaha ilallaah (There is no Ilaah which is deserving of worship/subservience except Allaah), the truth and certainty of which every Messenger came to establish. Allaah, the Mighty and Majestic, says:

Your Ilaah is but one Ilaah.
[Soorah an-Nahl (16):20]

And He alone is the Ilaah (of those) in the Heavens and the Ilaah (of those) in the Earth.
[Soorah az-Zukhruf (43):84].

Invoke not, or pray to any Ilaah along with Allaah. There is no Ilaah but He.
[Soorah Qasas (28):88].

[29] Ruboobiyyah: A term denoting the absolute sovereignty and kingship of Allaah over the heavens and the earth and whatever is between them. It has three aspects to it:

(i)   Khalq (creativity): Allaah by Himself makes everything from nothing.
(ii)   Mulk (possession): Allaah by Himself owns everything and
(iii)   Amr (administration): Allaah by Himself, controls and directs everything that He creates and all that He owns. Some of the proofs for these are:

He has the creation and His is the command/administration. Blessed be Allaah the Rabb of all Creation.
[Soorah al-A'raaf (7):54].

Allaah is your Rabb. He owns everything and those whom you call upon besides Him do not own even the white stringy strand on a date-stone (such a minute possession).
[Soorah Faatir (35):13].

Then the caller, with the speech of Allaah, "Guide us to the Straight Path..." realises his extreme need for this (guidance). He is never in need of any other thing as much as he is of this guidance. He is in need of it in every moment and at every glance of the eye.

Then Allaah makes it clear that the people of this Guidance are those who have been specified with His favour, not those upon whom is His anger, these latter ones are they who know the Truth but do not follow it, not those who are astray, and who worship Allaah without knowledge. Both of these groups share with each other in speaking about His creation, His command and His Names and Attributes without knowledge. The path of those upon whom is His favour and blessing is different from that of the people of falsehood with respect to knowledge and action.

When he finishes from this praise, supplication and tawheed, he has been ordered to end it with `aameen' which is a seal (to his supplication) and with which the aameen of the angels in the sky coincides. This aameen is from the beautification of the prayer, just like the raising of the hands is a beautification of the prayer, a following of the sunnah, veneration of the command of Allaah, worship by the hands and a sign of the transition from one pillar (of the prayer) to another.' [Taken from As-Salaatu wa Hukmu Taarikihaa, pp.171~172].

Chapter SIX

IBN QUDAAMAH AL-MAQDISEE AND HIS COMMENTS ON THE PRAYER[30]

He (may Allaah have mercy on him) said, "And know that the prayer has actions which are pillars, actions which are obligatory and actions which are sunnah. The spirit of prayer is in the niyyah (intention), ikhlaas (sincerity), khushoo' (awe coupled with humility and submissiveness) and the presence of the heart. The prayer also contains remembrances, private conversations (with Allaah) and physical actions. When the heart is not present the desired goal is not obtained by the remembrances and private conversations with Allaah, the Exalted. Because speech, when it does not express the innermost feelings or what is in the heart, is (nothing but) absent-mindedness and folly.

Likewise the desired goal (from the prayer) is not obtained from the (mere performance of) actions. The purpose of the standing in prayer is service (to Allaah) and the purpose of the rukoo' and sujood is magnification of Allaah and humility to Him. If the heart is not present, the desired goal will not be reached. When an action is devoid of the purpose and intent behind it, nothing remains except a picture or an impression which has no value to it. Allaah, the Exalted, said:

It is not the meat or blood (of the sacrifice) which reaches Allaah but it is the taqwaa (which is in your hearts) that reaches Him. [Soorah al_Hajj (22):37].

The meaning here is that what reaches Allaah is the quality which has overtaken and is predominant in the heart, so that this same feeling is present when the requested acts of worship are performed. It is vital that the heart is present. Allaah has, however, overlooked the unmindfulness which occurs unexpectedly in the prayer because the judgement for maintaining the presence of the heart at the beginning of the prayer continues for the rest of it.

---

[30] In his book Mukhtasir Minhaajil-Qaasideen, pp.29~32.

The meanings by which the life of the prayer is perfected are many.

The First: The presence of the heart as we have just mentioned. Its meaning is that the heart is empty and devoid of what is otherwise mixed with it. The cause of that is ambition and aspiration. When a matter is on your mind and concerns you, the heart will by necessity become engaged with it. There is nothing to cure this except to turn all your concerns towards the prayer (alone). A person's concerns in the prayer intensify and weaken in accordance with the strength of his eemaan in the Hereafter and the extent to which he holds the world in contempt. If you find that your heart is not present during the prayer then know that the reason for it is weak eemaan, so you must strive to strengthen it.

The Second: Understanding the meaning of the words and this is the matter which lies behind the presence of the heart. It may be that the heart is present with the pronunciation of the words but not with the meanings behind them. So it is desirable that the mind is turned towards perceiving their meanings by repelling other distracting thoughts and cutting off their roots because unless roots are cut off the thoughts continue to arise from them.

The root can either be external, such as what occupies the hearing and sight, or internal and this is stronger, like the one whose concerns for the world have multiplied and diversified. His thoughts are not restricted to one matter and even lowering his gaze does not protect him from this because whatever occurs in his heart is enough to keep him occupied.

If the root is external the cure for it is to cut off what occupies the hearing and the seeing and this includes being close to the qiblah (i.e., sutrah), looking at the place of prostration, being careful of and avoiding places which are colourful or attractive and not leaving anything besides oneself which would occupy his perceptions and feelings. The Prophet (ρ) when he prayed in a shirt which had marks upon it took it off and said, **"It has just diverted me from my prayer."**

If the root is internal, the way to treat it is to compel the soul to become occupied with what one is reciting in the prayer. He should prepare for that before entering the prayer by freeing himself from (thinking about all) other occupations, striving to empty his heart (from everything but the prayer), to renew the remembrance of the hereafter in his soul, realise the seriousness of standing in front of Allaah, the Mighty and Majestic, and the terror of being examined. If these are not the thoughts present (in the prayer) then a person should know that (his heart) is reflecting about those things which produce aspirations and desires in him. Let him therefore leave those desires and cut off those attachments.

Know that when an illness sets in and becomes firm nothing but strong medicine can repel it. When an illness intensifies it competes with the one who prays and the one who prays competes with it until the prayer expires in this competition.

The example of this is of a man who is sitting under a tree, trying to devote himself to thinking and reflecting, but then birds disturb and confuse him. So he tries to make them fly away with the stick which is in his hand. He then thinks and (deep thought) has not yet lodged into his mind when the birds come back. It is said to him, "This thing cannot be prevented. If you want it to stop then cut the tree down." This tree is the desire. When it becomes sick (corrupted) and its branches become numerous, thoughts and ideas are drawn towards it just like birds drawn towards a tree and flies towards dirt and filth. So one's precious life is spent in repelling what cannot be repelled. The cause of this desire which brings about these thoughts and ideas is love of the world.

It was said to 'Aamir ibn 'Abd Qais (may Allaah have mercy on him), "Do you converse with your soul about anything from the matters of the world during prayer?" He said, "That my teeth become twisted is better to me than that I find this." Know that cutting off the love of the world from the heart is a difficult matter and to completely prevent it is a mighty task. Let him then strive in whatever is possible and Allaah is the One Who gives support and aid.

The Third: Magnification of Allaah and awe/reverence of Him. This occurs by two things. Cognition of the Majesty and Grandeur of Allaah, the Exalted, and cognition of the insignificance of the soul and the fact that it causes one to become enslaved. This cognition occurs by two things, willing submission/yielding (Istikaanah) and awe coupled with humility and submission (khushoo').

Included within this is hope as it is an addition to one's fear. How many venerated kings are there who are feared because of their authority and influence just as hope is placed in them for their benevolence? It is desirable, therefore, for the worshipper to hope for reward for his prayer and to fear punishment for his negligence.

It is also desirable for the worshipper to make his heart present during all the matters which are related to the prayer. When he hears the call of the mu'adhdhin he should liken it to the call on the Day of Judgement and set out to answer it with vigour and determination. Let him consider (the reality of) what he is responding to and in what state his body comes to the prayer.

When he has covered himself (for the prayer) he should realise that the purpose behind it is to conceal the shamefulness of his body from the creation. Let him also realise his deficiencies and defects and the scandals and disgraces of his inner self which none can know except the Creator and which none can cover or hide. Only remorse, modesty and fear can expiate for them.

When he faces the qiblah he has turned his face from all other directions to the direction of the House of Allaah and yet turning his heart to Allaah is more befitting than that. Just as he cannot face the qiblah without turning away from all else besides it, likewise the heart cannot turn to Allaah without turning away from all that is besides Him.

When you make the takbeer (i.e., say, 'Allaahu Akbar), O worshipper, do not let your heart treat your tongue as having lied, because if there is something greater than Allaah in your heart then you have lied. Beware also that your whim and desire is greater (than Allaah) which would be proven by your preference to go along with it (rather) than to give obedience to Allaah, the Exalted.

When you seek refuge, know that seeking refuge means recourse to Allaah, the Sublime. When you do not seek refuge with your heart (as well), then your words are futile and ineffective.

Understand the meaning of what you recite. Make this understanding present with your heart when you say:
All praise belongs to Allaah the Rabb of all the Worlds.

Bring to mind His Benevolence when you say:
The Most Gracious, the Most Merciful.

And His Might and Grandeur when you say:
Master of the Day of Judgement.

And likewise (understand the meaning) of everything that you recite.

We have already reported about Zuraarah ibn Abee 'Awfaa (may Allaah have mercy on him) that when he recited in his prayer:

And when the Trumpet is blown (a second time).

he fell to the ground, dead. This did not occur except that he imagined and pictured that situation and it brought destruction upon him.

Try to feel modesty in your bowing and humility in your prostration because in such a position you have placed the soul in its proper place. In the prostration you have returned the limbs to their place of origin, upon the dust from which they were created. Understand also the meaning of the remembrances with inclination and zeal.

Know that performing the prayer with these internal conditions is a cause-of the purity of the heart from adulteration and pollution, of obtaining the light by which the Might and Greatness of the One Who is worshipped is realised and of discovering His secrets and none understands them except those grounded in knowledge (the scholars).

As for the one who is standing performing the external actions without knowing their significance or meanings he will not realise or discover any of the above, rather he will reject its existence.

Chapter Seven

THE VARIOUS POSTURES OF THE PRAYER[31]

An Explanation of What should be Present in the Heart During every Pillar and Moment from the Actions of the Prayer

And these are the Call to Prayer, purification, covering ones awrah, facing the qiblah, standing, the intention, the takbeer, seeking refuge, the basmalah, the recitation of Faatihah and another soorah, the rukoo, sujood and tashahhud.

The Call to Prayer (Aadhaan)
When you hear the Call to Prayer then make the terror of the call on the Day of judgement present in your heart and prepare yourself externally and internally to respond and race towards it. Those who race to answer this call are the ones who will be called out with benevolence on the Day of Judgement. Remember also the description which Allaah, the Mighty and Majestic, has given to the Hypocrites when he said:

And when they stand for the prayer they stand without earnestness (lazily). [Soorah an-Nisaa (4):142].

The description of the Believers is the opposite of that. They stand for the prayer whilst rejoicing and with eagerness and liveliness, turning themselves towards Allaah, the Mighty and Majestic.

The Purification
Then you purify yourself in your home which is the furthest place (from the place of prayer), then your clothes which are your nearest covering and then your skin which is your lowest and innermost covering do not forget to purify your heart with repentance, remorse, firm resolution not to return to sins, and avoiding

---

[31] Risaalah Ta'dheem Qadr is-Salaat of Ahmad Fareed, pp.69~77.

injustices (to others). The purification of the inner self precedes the purification of the external form.

Covering One's Awrah
Its meaning is that you conceal the undesirable parts of the body from the creation, but bring to mind along with this the ugly traits and characteristics and the scandals of your inner self. Try to bring about modesty and feel shameful in front of Allaah, the Mighty and Majestic, from Whom no secret is hidden, as it is not possible to cover it.

Facing the Qiblah
This is turning your face away from all other directions to the direction of the House of Allaah, the Mighty and Majestic. Know that it is also obligatory to turn the heart away from all other things towards Allaah, the Mighty and Majestic. Thus there occurs in one of the opening supplications of the prayer, "I have turned my face towards the One Who Created the heavens and the earth, sincerely." The purpose is the turning of the heart towards Allaah and its sincerity towards Him after the body has been made to face the House of Allaah.

The Standing
This is making the body and the heart stand erect, upright in front of Allaah, the Mighty and Majestic. Bring to mind along with this the standing in front of Allaah on the Day of judgement for questioning and try to feel and sense the Might of Allaah, the Mighty and Majestic. Prepare yourself to stand in front of Him (in prayer) in such a way that it will lead you to safety on the Day of Judgement.

The Intentions
Fill your intention with sincerity to Allaah, the Mighty and Majestic, hoping for His reward, fearing His punishment and loving His nearness. Train and nurture yourself to recall this sincere intention along with every speech and action and know that none will be saved on the Day of judgement except the sincere ones. Every action which has a desire for other than Allaah is adulterated and obscured. Allaah, the Mighty and Majestic, said regarding this:

And We shall turn to whatever actions they did and make them into scattered dust. [Soorah al_Furqaan (25):23].

The Takbeer

When you declare the takbeer with your tongue it is desirable that your heart does not treat it as having lied. If there is something in your heart which is greater than Allaah, the Sublime, or if your whim and desire is greater to you than Allaah, the Mighty and Majestic, and you are more obedient to it than to Allaah, the Exalted-then you have taken it as a god and you will have declared its greatness. So your saying, "Allaah is Greater," will have been but a mere expression of the tongue and the heart will have refrained from supporting the tongue. If it had not been for repentance, seeking forgiveness and harbouring good thoughts about Allaah's generosity and forgiveness, this would have been one of the greatest dangers.

Seeking Refuge

Know that this means seeking a sanctuary with Allaah, the Mighty, from Satan, the Rejected and Accursed-the one who lies in wait for you, jealous of your private conversation with your Lord, the Mighty and Majestic, and of your bowing and prostration to Him, together with the fact that Satan did not agree to or offer a single prostration to Him. He has made it his concern to prevent you and cut you off from conversing privately with your Lord by his whisperings about the concerns and affairs of the world and its engagements and occupations until he prevents you from the honour of secretly conversing with Allaah, its blessing and its reward. He also tries to cut you off from your Master, whose love and secret conversations make the hearts happy, and from gaining nobility in this life and the Hereafter by His remembrance and beautiful worship.

The Basmalah

When you pronounce this, intend to receive blessings by the name of Allaah along with which nothing in the heavens or the earth can cause harm, He is the All_Hearing the All-Knowing. When you say Ar-Rahmaanir-Raheem, recall in your heart His various benevolences so that His Mercy becomes manifest to you and hope arises in your heart.

Recitation of the Faatihah

Remember the saying of the Messenger (ρ), that he has narrated from his Lord, "I have divided the Prayer between Myself and My servant into two halves, and My servant shall have what he has asked for. When the servant says:

All praise belongs to Allaah the Rabb of all the Worlds.
Allaah, the Mighty and Majestic, says, "My servant has praised Me." And when he says:

The Most Gracious, the Most Merciful.
Allaah, the Mighty and Majestic, says, "My servant has extolled Me." And when he says:

Master of the Day of Judgement.
Allaah, the Mighty and Majestic, says, "My servant has glorified Me..." and on one occasion He said, "My servant has submitted to My power." And when he says:

You alone do we worship and from You alone do we seek help.
He says, "This is between Me and My servant, and My servant shall have what he has asked for." And when he says:

Guide us to the Straight Path, the Path of those whom You have favoured, not of those upon whom is Your anger, nor of those who are astray.
He says, "This is for My servant, and My servant shall have what he has asked for.""

An-Nawawi (may Allaah have mercy on him) said, "The scholars have said, 'And the meaning of the word 'prayer' (in this hadeeth) is the Faatihah.'"

(His saying), 'I have divided it ...' is in terms of its meaning because the first half of it contains praise of Allaah, His glorification, extolling Him and submitting (one's affairs) to Him and the second half contains a request, an imploration and a need.

Al-Qaasimee (may Allaah have mercy on him) said, "These meanings are related to the levels of understanding and the levels of understanding are related to the abundance of knowledge and the clarity of the heart. The levels and degrees of this (amongst people) cannot be comprehended. The prayer is the key to the hearts. Within it, the secrets of the words (which are recited) are uncovered. This is the right of the recitation and is also the right of the remembrances, and the glorifications. Then the worshipper should observe and maintain awe and fear of Allaah during his recitation by reciting with slow rhythmic tones (Tarteel) as this makes it easier to reflect."

The Bowing and the Prostration

Ibn Qudaamah (may Allaah have mercy on him) said, "Try to feel modesty in your bowing and humility in your prostration because in such a position you have placed the soul in its proper place. In prostration you have returned the limbs to their place of origin-upon the dust from which they were created. Understand also the meaning of the remembrances with inclination and zeal."

Al-Qaasimee (may Allaah have mercy on him) said, "It is desirable that you renew the mention of the Greatness of Allaah, the Sublime, during them, that you strive to soften your heart, renew your khushoo' and that you sense and realise the power of your Master and His transcendency, then your own lowliness and insignificance. Seek help from Allaah to establish all of that in your heart and upon your tongue. Glorify Allaah (above all defects) then give testimony for His Grandeur and that He is Mightier than every single thing. Repeat this so that it is confirmed and established (in your heart).

By saying, "Allaah listens to the one who praises Him..." which means He will respond to the one who is grateful to Him, you raise your head from the bowing with certain hope. Then follow that with additional gratefulness by saying, "O Lord! To You belongs all praise." Then fall into prostration which is the highest form of submission and yielding oneself (to Allaah). Place and fix the noblest of your limbs, the face, upon the lowest of things, the dust. Along with this renew in your heart the greatness of Allaah and say, "Glorified is my Lord the Highest," then raise your head while declaring His greatness and asking Him for your need by saying, "O Lord! Forgive me and show mercy to me." Confirm your modesty and humility by repeating this a number of times and then return to the prostration for a second time.

This then, is the explanation of the prayer of the khaashi'een those who are humble and submissive in their prayers, the ones who guard their prayers, the ones who are constant in offering them, the ones who converse with Allaah to the extent that they are able to become enslaved to Him. Let the worshipper turn himself to this prayer, let him rejoice to the extent to which it has been made easy for him and let him be grieved to the extent that the prayer has passed him by, and let him strive to find the cure for that.

As for the prayer of the inattentive and heedless, it is very risky, unless Allaah covers him with His Mercy and Allaah's Mercy is vast and His Generosity is abounding. We ask Allaah that He covers us with His Mercy and that He showers us with His forgiveness as there is no way for us except to admit our incapacity to perform His obedience.

Chapter Eight

THE LEVELS OF PEOPLE WITH REGARD TO THEIR PRAYER[32]

Ibn al-Qayyim (may Allaah have mercy on him) said, "And mankind, with regard to their performance of prayer are in five levels.

The First: The level of the one who is negligent and wrongs his soul. He is the one who falls short in performing ablution properly, performing the prayer upon its time and within its specified limits, and in fulfilling its essential pillars.

The Second: The one who guards his prayers upon their proper times and within their specified limits, fulfils their essential pillars and performs his ablution with care. However, his striving (in achieving the above) is wasted due to whisperings in his prayer so he is taken away by thoughts and ideas.

The Third: The one who guards his prayers within the specified limits, fulfils their essential pillars and strives with himself to repel the whisperings, thoughts and ideas. He is busy struggling against his enemy (Satan) so that he does not steal from the prayer. On account of this he is engaged in (both) prayer and jihaad.

The Fourth: The one who stands for the prayer, completes and perfects its due rights, its essential pillars, performs it within its specified limits and his heart becomes engrossed in safeguarding its rights and specified limits, so that nothing is wasted from it. His whole concern is directed towards its establishment, its completion and its perfection, as it should be. His heart is immersed in the prayer and in enslavement to his Lord, the Exalted.

The Fifth: The one who stands for the prayer like the one mentioned above. However, on top of this, he has taken and placed his heart in front of his Lord, the Mighty and Majestic, looking towards Him with his heart with anticipation, (his heart) filled with His love and His might, as if he sees and witnesses Allaah. The

---

[32] Al-Waabilus-Sayyib, pp.23~24.

whisperings, thoughts and ideas have vanished and the coverings which are between him and his Lord are raised. What is between this person and others with respect to the prayer, is superior and greater than what is between the heavens and the earth. This person is busy with his Lord, the Mighty and Majestic, delighted with Him.

The first type will be punished, **the second** type will be held to account, **the third** will have his sins and shortcomings expiated, **the fourth** will be rewarded and **the fifth** will be close to his Lord, because he will receive the portion of the one who makes his prayer the delight and pleasure of his eye. Whoever makes his prayer the delight and pleasure of his eye, will have the nearness to his Lord, the Mighty and Majestic, made the delight and pleasure of his eye in the hereafter. He will also be made a pleasure to the eye in this world since whoever makes Allaah the pleasure of his eye in this world, every other eye will become delighted and pleased with him.

Chapter Nine

A SUMMARY OF THE LESSONS AND BENEFITS OF PRAYER[33]

(1) That Allaah, the Exalted, wipes away sins by the five prayers.

(2) That the five prayers are an expiation for what occurs between them, if major sins are avoided.

(3) That sins burn and destroy a person and thus it is necessary to extinguish that with the prayers.

(4) That the Muslim reaches the level of the truthful and the martyrs on account of his prayers, charity and fasting.

(5) The superiority of prayer[34] over other actions.

(6) That Allaah, the Exalted, bestowed a favour upon that Companion by entering him into Paradise before his brother who died as a martyr because he prayed more than he.

(7) That the prayer is light which illuminates the path of the servant in this world and the Hereafter.

(8) That an abundance of prostrations and prayers is the way to accompany the Messenger (ρ) in Paradise.

(9) That a two rak'ah prayer is more loved by the dead person than the world and whatever is in it.

(10) That emptying the heart for Allaah in the prayer puts a person in the same condition as the day when his mother gave birth to him.

(11) That should a person enter the Fire, refuge is sought from that, the angels will remove him from it and will recognise him by the marks of prostration.[35]

(12) That the prayer participates in undoing the knots which Satan places at the top of ones head.

(13) That the night prayer is the most excellent prayer after the obligatory prayers.

(14) That the one who prays at night obtains a reward which most of mankind do not.

---

[33] Summarised from Hussain al-Awaa'ishah's, As-Salaat, wa Atharuhaa fee Ziyaadatil Eemaan wa Tahdheeb in-Nafs.

[34] Its condition is that the creed of the person is correct, sound and in accordance with that of the Pious Predecessors of this Ummah.

[35] The condition for being removed from the Fire due to the intercession of the angels (and others) is that a person should be from the People of Tawheed. Intercession is only for the People of Tawheed.

(15) Gratitude is shown to Allaah with the (obligatory) prayer and night prayer.

(16) That the prayer most loved by Allaah is the prayer of Daawood (υ) which is to pray for a third of the night and to sleep for two thirds of the night.[36]

(17) That as Allaah has bestowed a favour upon His servant by the hour during the night in which the supplication is answered, it is befitting for the Muslim to aspire to it and seek to find it so that he is given the good of this world and the Hereafter.

(18) That the night prayer is an evidence for righteousness and taqwaa and it expiates the sins and prevents one from falling into them.

(19) That Allaah, the Mighty and Majestic, covers the husband and wife who help each other in performing the night prayer with His Mercy. If one of them refuses the other sprinkles water on his or her face.

(20) That two units of prayer at night make a person amongst the men who remember Allaah often or the women who remember Allaah often.

(21) That Allaah is amazed by the man who gets up from his sleep, leaving his bedsheet, his wife and his love for her in order to perform prayer. Allaah laughs because of him and informs the angels about him.

(22) That there is no jealousy or competition except with regard to two men, one of whom prays at night reciting the Qur'aan which Allaah has bestowed upon him.

(23) That whoever recited ten aayaat in the night (in prayer) will not be written amongst the heedless, a Qintaar of reward will be written for him and Allaah, the Exalted, will say to him, "Recite and rise by one degree with every aayah," until he comes to the last aayah he knows. Allaah favours him by giving him eternity.

(24) That whoever prays at night with a hundred aayaat is written amongst the devout worshippers and whoever prays with a thousand aayaat is written amongst the Muqantareen and whoever prays with two hundred aayaat is written amongst the devout worshippers and sincere ones.

(25) That the one who walks to the prayer (in the mosque) is raised in ranks and has his sins removed, both while he goes to the mosque and when he returns from it.

---

[36] Due to his (ρ) saying, "... he used to sleep half the night, then prayer for a third and then go to sleep for a sixth of it." A half added to a sixth is two-thirds.

(26) That for every step he takes he receives ten good deeds.

(27) That the Muslim is written amongst the worshippers from the time he leaves the house till he returns to it.

(28) That the one receiving the greatest reward for the prayer is the one who walks the furthest towards it and then the one further than him (from the mosque).

(29) That one step which a servant takes to the prayer in congregation is counted as an act of charity for him.

(30) That taking many steps towards the mosque is from ar-Ribaat (guarding the frontiers).

(31) That every time a servant leaves for the mosque in the morning or the evening Allaah prepares for him a feast in Paradise.

(32) That Allaah makes the light of those who walk through the darkness to the mosques complete and perfect on the Day of Judgement.

(33) That the reward for the one who leaves his house in a state of purity for the obligatory prayer is like the reward of the pilgrim in the state of ihraam.

(34) That the one who leaves for the mosque has a guarantee from Allaah that He should provide sustenance for him and suffice him (in his affairs).

(35) That the one who walks for the prayer in congregation, after having beautified his ablution and travels to visit Allaah, the Exalted, is bestowed with a great favour in that Allaah honours those of his servants who visit Him, and Allaah's honouring of them is increasing their faith, showing benevolence to them, rewarding them, raising their ranks, removing their difficulties and making their hearts content and happy.

(36) The obligation to pray in congregation.

(37) That the Prophet (ρ) did not make a concession for the old blind man by allowing him to leave the congregational prayer. How then can those who are fit and well be allowed a concession?

(38) That whoever abandons the congregational prayer has been threatened with heedlessness and having a seal placed on his heart.

(39) That staying away from the congregational prayer is a sign of hypocrisy.

(40) The extreme striving of the Companions (ψ) for attending the congregational prayer inspite of difficult circumstances. Some of the Salaf used to say, **"The prayer is from the Hereafter so when you enter it you leave the world."**

Chapter Ten

THE METHODOLOGY OF A MUSLIM

Know, may Allaah have mercy upon you, that the methodology a Muslim adopts in reaching his Lord, safe and secure, is suspended between two matters.

(i)   Holding fast to the Sunnah and its people, its aiders, allies and supporters and
(ii)   avoiding all innovation, its people, its aiders, allies and supporters, those "deceiving, surmising, cheating, lying, beautifiers of speech."[37] This is the Straight Path of Allaah, that which leads to Him and in which there is no crookedness, neither to the left, nor to the right.

Imaam as-Shaatibee (may Allaah have mercy on him) said, "And 'Umar ibn Salamah al-Hamdaanee said, 'We were sitting in the circle of Ibn Mas'ood in the mosque, which was still plain ground, before it had been covered with gravel. 'Ubaidullaah ibn 'Umar ibn al-Khattaab, who had just returned from an expedition, said to him, 'What is the straight path, O Aboo 'Abdur-Rahmaan? 'He replied, 'By the Lord of the Ka'bah, it is that which your father was firmly established upon until he entered Paradise,' and then he swore firmly upon that three times. Then he drew a line in the ground with his hand and also drew lines to either side of it and said, 'Your Prophet (ρ) left you upon this end and its other end is in Paradise. So whoever remains steadily upon it will enter Paradise and whoever takes any of these lines will be destroyed."

And in another narration (he was asked), 'O Aboo 'Abdur-Rahmaan, what is the straight path?' He said, 'The Messenger (ρ) left us upon the nearest end of the line and its other end is in Paradise. And to its left and right are roads in which there are men who invite those who pass by them, saying, 'Come this way! Come this way!' So whoever is taken by them to those paths will end up in Hell-Fire and whoever remains steadfast upon the great path will end up, through it, in Paradise.' Then Ibn Mas'ood recited:

---

[37] The saying of Aboo Haatim ar-Raazee (d. 264H) as quoted by al-Laalikaa'ee in Sharh Usoolul-I'tiqaad Ahlus-Sunnah wal-Jamaa'ah (2/176~182).

And verily, this is my Straight Path, so follow it, and follow not (other) paths, for they will separate you away from His Path. This He has ordained for you that you may become al-Muttaqoon." [Soorah al-Anam (6):153].

And Mujaahid said about the saying of Allaah, **"...and follow not (other) paths.."** "The innovations and doubts." And Bakr ibn al-Alaa said about the saying of Allaah, **"... for they will separate you away from His Path ..."** "He meant the devils amongst men, and these are the innovations and Allaah knows best." [Imaam ash-Shaatibee in Al-I'tisaam (1/40~45)].

The Aider of the Sunnah and Destroyer of Innovations, Imaarn Ahmad (d.241 H) (may Allaah have mercy on him) said, "The fundamental principles of the Sunnah with us are:

(i) Holding fast to what the Companions of Allaah's Messenger (ρ) were upon.
(ii) Seeking them (and their way) as a model of guidance.
(iii) Abandoning innovation, for every innovation is misguidance.
(iv) Abandoning controversies and abandoning sitting with the People of Desires.
(v) And abandoning quarrelling, argumentation and controversies in the religion."[Reported by al-Laalikaa'ee in his Sharh Usoolul-I'tiqaad (1/152)].

Aboo Haneefah (d.159H) (may Allaah have mercy on him) said, "Stick to the narration (athar) and the way of the Salaf and beware of newly invented matters, for all of it is innovation." [Related by as-Suyootee in Sawnul- Mantaq wal-Kalaam (p.32)].

Imaam al-Awzaa'ee (d.157H) (may Allaah have mercy on him) said, "Hold fast to the narrations of the Salaf, even if people were to abandon you. Beware of the opinions of the people, no matter how much they beautify it with their speech." [Related by al-Khateeb al-Baghdadee in his Sharaf Ashaabul-Hadeeth (p.7)].

And Imaam al-Laalikaa'ee (d.418H) (may Allaah have mercy on him) said, "That which is most obligatory upon a Muslim is knowledge of the aspects of the creed of the Religion and what

Allaah has obligated upon His Servants including the understanding of His Tawheed and of His Attributes, and believing in His Messengers with evidences and with certainty. And arriving at (all of) that and seeking evidences for them with clear proofs.

Among the mightiest of statements and clearest of proofs and understandings is:

(i)   The Book of Allah, the Manifest Truth.
(ii)   Then the saying of the Messenger of Allaah (p).
(iii)   And of his Companions, the Chosen, pious ones.
(iv)   Then that which the Salafus-Saalih were unanimously agree upon.
(v)   Hen holding fast of all of that and remaining firm upon it till he Day of Judgement.
(vi)   Then turning away from the innovations and from listening to them-from amongst those things the astray people have invented." [Sharh Usool-I'tiqaad (1/9)].

Therefore, "May Allaah have mercy upon you! Examine carefully the speech of speech of everyone you hear from in your time particularly. So do not act in haste and do not enter into anything from it until you ask and see-'Did any of the Companions of the Prophet (p) speak about it or any of the scholars?" So if you find a narration from them, cling to it, do not go beyond it for anything and do not give precedence to anything over it and thus fall into the fire." [Sharh-Sunnah of Imaam al-Barbahaaree].

Chapter Eleven

IBN AL-QAYYIM ON FOLLOWING A SCHOOL OF THOUGHT (MADHHAB)

Ibn al-Qayyim said, "Does the common person have to follow one of the well-known madhhabs or not? There are two sayings regarding this:

That it is not obligatory upon him and this is what is correct and definite since there is nothing obligatory except what Allaah, the Most High, and His Messenger have made obligatory. Neither Allaah nor His Messenger made it obligatory to follow the school of thought (madhhab) of any person from the ummah and to follow him alone in the Religion. The best generations passed by without anyone doing this. Indeed the common person cannot have a madhhab, even if he thinks that he does, since the common person has no madhhab at all. This is because the madhhab will be either for the one who is able to research to a certain level and understand evidence and also know about the other madhhabs or for the one who has read a book concerning the details of that madhhab and knows the ruling and sayings of his Imaam.

As for the one who is unable to do any of that but merely says, 'I am a Shaafi'ee ...' or 'I am Hanbalee ...' etc., then he does not become that just by saying so, just as would be the case if he said, 'I am a religious scholar ...' or 'I am a scholar of grammar ...' or 'I am a writer ...' then he does not become that just by saying so. This is further clarified by the fact that the one who says, 'I am a Shaafi'ee ... or a Maalikee ... or a Hanafee ...' claiming that he follows that Imaam and his way, would only be truthful if he were to follow his way in acquiring knowledge, understanding and extraction of proof. As for this one, with his ignorance and being far from the manners of the Imaam and his knowledge and way, how can it be correct for him to ascribe himself to him except with mere claims and empty words having no meaning?! How can the common person have a madhhab? Even if it could be imagined, it would still not be obligatory upon him or anyone else to ever have to follow the madhhab of a certain man from the ummah, to the extent that he accepts all his sayings and rejects everyone else's sayings.

This is a filthy innovation introduced into the ummah.

No scholar of Islaam has ever said this and they are higher in station and better knowing about Allaah than to order the people about this. Even further from the truth is the saying of those who say that he must stick to the madhhab of a single scholar and further still from the truth is the one who says, he must follow one of the four madhhabs! O Allaah, how strange!

(Is it that) the madhhabs of the Companions of Allaah's Messenger (ρ) died out and those of the taabi'een and those who came after them and those of the rest of the scholars of Islaam and all have been invalidated except for the madhhabs of four men only from amongst all the rest of the scholars and Imaams?!

Rather, that which Allaah, the Most High, and His Messenger (ρ) made obligatory upon the Companions, the taabi'een and those who came after them is the same as that which He made obligatory upon those after them until the Day of Resurrection. That which is obligatory does not vary or change, even though how it is achieved may vary or the amount which is obligatory may vary due to varying ability or inability, time, place and condition, but that also follows what Allaah and His Messenger have obligated.

Those who say that it is correct for the common person to have a madhhab claim, 'Because he believes that the madhhab which he ascribes himself to is the truth, therefore, he must be sincere to his belief.' If this saying of theirs were true then it would mean that it is forbidden to seek a ruling from anyone other than the people of his own madhhab and likewise that it is forbidden to take the madhhab of anyone equal or greater than his own Imaam and would mean other things which all show the falsity of the belief in the first place. Indeed it would mean that if he saw a text from Allaah's Messenger (ρ) or a saying from the four Caliphs with other than his own Imaam, he would have to abandon the text and the sayings of the Companions and give precedence to the saying of his own Imaam.

Rather, he should seek from whom he wishes from the followers of the four madhhabs and others besides them. It is not obligatory upon him or upon the one who delivers verdicts (muftee) to limit himself to one of the four Imaams. Upon this is the consensus of the ummah, just as it is not obligatory upon the scholar to restrict himself to the hadeeths reported by the people of his land or any land in particular, rather, if any hadeeth is authentic it is obligatory to act upon it,[38] whether it is reported of the people of the Hijaaz, Iraaq, Shaam, Egypt or Yemen." [I'laamul-Muwaqqi'een (4/261)].

---

[38] Aboo Haneefah (may Allaah have mercy on him) said, "When I say something contradicting the Book of Allaah, the Exalted, or what is narrated from the Messenger (r), then ignore my saying," al-Fulaani in Eeqaaz al-Himam (p.50), tracing it to Imaam Muhammad and then saying, "This does not apply to the mujtahid, for he is not bound to their views anyway, but it applies to the blind-following." Imaam Maalik (may Allaah have mercy on him) said, "Truly I am only a mortal. I make mistakes (sometimes) and I am correct (sometimes). Therefore, look into my opinions, all that agrees with the Book and the Sunnah, accept it. And all that does not agree with the Book and the Sunnah, ignore it" Ibn 'Abdul-Barr in Jaami' Bayaanal-Ilm (2/32). Imaam ash-Shaafi'ee (may Allaah have mercy on him) said, "The sunnahs of the Messenger of Allaah (r), reach, as well as escape from, every one of us. So whenever I voice my opinion or formulate a principle, where something contrary to my view exists on the authority of the Messenger of Allaah (r), then the correct view is what the Messenger of Allaah (r) has said-and it is my view," related by Haakim with a continuous chain of narration up to Shaafi'ee, as in Taareekh Dimashq of Ibn 'Asaakir (15/1/3), I'laamul-Muwaqqi'een (2/363,364). And he also said, "The Muslims are unanimously agreed that if a sunnah of the Messenger of Allaah (r) is made clear to someone, it is not permitted for him to leave it for the saying of anyone else." Ibn al-Qayyim (2/361) and Fulaani (p.68). Imaam Ahmad said, "The opinion of Awzaa'ee, the opinion of Maalik, the opinion of Aboo Haneefah-all of it is opinion, and it is all equal in my eyes. However, the proof is in the narrations (from the Prophet (r) and his Companions)," Ibn 'Abdul-Barr in Jaami' Bayaan al'-Ilm (2/149).

Chapter Twelve

IBN ALQAYYIM ON MAKING USE OF ONE'S TIME IN CHANGING EVIL INTO GOOD[39]

Abdul-Malik ibn Ahmad al-Mubaarak said, "Ibn al-Qayyim (may Allaah have mercy on him) said in AL-Fawaa'id, "Chapter: How you rectify your condition:

"Get up (and hurry) in entering upon Allaah and accompanying Him in the Home of Peace, without any tiredness, hardship or fatigue, but in fact by the nearest of paths and the most easiest (of them). And this is (by realising) that you are in a time between two times which is (what constitutes) your life, and this is the present time which is between what has passed and what is yet to come. Then that which has passed, you can correct by repentance, remorse and seeking forgiveness. This is something in which there will be no tiredness, fatigue, or any straining efforts (required on your behalf). It is (nothing but) the action of the heart.'"

"I say: Whatever of your time has passed in disobedience to Allaah, it is possible for you to bring it back (and amend it). And it has been said, 'Time is like a sword, if you don't cut it, it will cut you.' And this is correct wisdom save that Allaah has excepted the repenters from this. For whatever time they have wasted in committing zinaa, even murder, in fact, even shirk-then whoever repents from them will find his scroll (of deeds) not just white and plain (free of those evils) but good deeds will have been written on it in replacement of those evil deeds, as if his time had been adorned with them. And nothing is impossible for Allaah, He is the One who said:

And those who invoke not any other ilaah (god) along with Allaah, nor kill such life as Allaah has forbidden, except for just cause, nor commit illegal sexual intercourse and

whoever does this shall receive the punishment. The torment will be doubled for him on the Day of Resurrection, and he will abide therein in disgrace. Except those who repent and believe, and do righteous deeds, for those, Allaah will change their sins into good deeds, and Allaah is Oft-Forgiving, Most Merciful." [Soorah al-Furqaan (25):68~70].

And Ibn al_Qayyim said:

"And your restraining yourself from sins in what has yet to come (in the future). (This) restraint of yours is but mere abandonment and relaxation and does not involve (any) actions from the limbs or the efforts which cause you difficulties and hardship. It is but (firm) resolution and a strong and firm intention (which allows your) body, heart and your inner-self to rest. So whatever has passed you by, you amend by repentance and you correct what has yet to come with restraint, resolution (of one's will) and (firm) intention."

"I say: From this you will learn about the secret of the connection between repentance and seeking forgiveness, as occurs in the like of Allaah's saying:

Will they not repent to Allaah and ask His Forgiveness? For Allaah is Oft-Forgiving, Most Merciful. [Soorah al-Maa'idah (5):135].

Seeking forgiveness (here) has the meaning of 'abandoning what has preceded (from your actions)' and repentance (here) is with the meaning 'not persisting (in those actions) in the future.' And Allaah has combined both of these in a single aayah when He said:

And those who, when they have committed faahishah (illegal sexual intercourse etc.,) or wronged themselves with evil, remember Allaah and ask forgiveness for their sins-and none can forgive sins but Allaah. And do not persist in what (wrong) they have done, while they know." Soorah Aali-Imran (3):135].

And Ibn al_Qayyim said:

"And in both of these there is no hardship or tiredness for the limbs, however the concern is for your life- and that is the time, (at present), which is between two times. If you waste it, you will have wasted your happiness and your (means of) safety. And if you safeguard it, along with correcting the (other) two times-that which is before it and that which comes after it-with what has been mentioned, you will be saved and you will succeed with ease, pleasure and bliss."

I say: And this will show you the secret of Allaah's making the amending of one's conduct (Islaah) a condition for (true) repentance, which if it (i.e., repentance) is performed (freely and properly), will also include the seeking of forgiveness, as occurs in the saying of Allaah:

Your Lord has written Mercy for Himself, so that, if any of you does evil in ignorance, and thereafter repents and does righteous good deeds (by obeying Allaah), then surely, He is Oft-Forgiving, Most Merciful. [Soorah al-An'aam (6):54].

and in His saying:

Except for those who repent after that and do righteous deeds. Verily, Allaah is Oft-Forgiving, Most Merciful. [Soorah Aali-'Imraan (3):89].

Therefore, amending one's conduct (here) is with the meaning of amending the present time (in which you are in), and it has been said:

"What has passed is a dream
And what is hoped for (in the future) is unseen
Yet you have (at your disposal)
The hour in which you are (at present)"

And Ibn al-Qayyim said:

"And safeguarding it involves greater hardship than the rectification of what has passed before it and what is to come after it. Safeguarding the present time requires that you make your soul cling to that which befits it, is of greater benefit to it and is greatest in obtaining its happiness. In this affair, people vary greatly one from another. Verily, these are your days gone past,[40] in which you gather your provision for your place of return, either to Paradise or to Hell-Fire..."

I say: Whoever contemplates over the Qur'aan will find that its call does not leave any of these three times. Allaah, the Exalted, said:

Alif, Laam, Raa. (This is) a Book, the aayaat whereof are perfected (in every sphere of knowledge) and then explained in detail from One, Who is All-Wise and Well, Acquainted (with all things). (Saying), 'Worship none but Allaah. Verily, I (Muhammad (ρ)) am unto you from Him a warner and a bringer of glad tidings.' And (commanding you), `Seek the forgiveness of your Lord, and turn to Him in repentance ...' [Soorah hood (11):1~3].

Meaning, that Allaah has perfected His Book and has explained it in detail that you may worship Him in these three times with what He has commanded. So His saying, **"(Saying) worship none but Allaah ..."** is for worship at the present time (in which you are in), for tawheed is the most beneficial and foremost of the acts of obedience. And His saying, **"And (commanding you), 'Seek the forgiveness of your Lord ...'"** is for what has passed, and His saying, **"And turn to Him in repentance ..."** is for what is to come.[41] The reason for concentrating upon tawheed here, for the rectification and correction of one's current time is two matters:

---

[40] Allaah, the Exalted said:
Then as for him who will be given his Record in his right hand, he will say, `Take, read my Record! Surely, I did believe that I shall meet my Account!' So he shall be in a life, well-Pleasing. In a lofty Paradise, the fruits in bunches whereof will be low and near at hand. `Eat and drink at ease for that which you have sent on before you in days past!' [Soorah al-Haaqqah (69): 19~24].

[41] This is one of the sayings by which `Istighfaar' and `Tawbah' have been explained, which have been mentioned in this aayah, as ash-Shawkaanee has quoted in Fathul-Qadeer (2/481). And this explanation which Ibn al-Qayyim has mentioned about the division of the three times is not the result of mere thinking, rather he has taken it (may

The first: That it is not permissible for there to be any time in which there is no concern with tawheed and it is that which comprises Tawheedur-Ruboobiyyah, Tawheedul-Uloohiyyah and Tawheedul-Asmaa was-Sifaat.

The second: That it is the foundation of every righteous action. Do you not see that righteous actions constitute its perfection, the obligatory amongst them or the recommended? For this reason it was the first thing that the Prophets, upon them be prayers and peace, called to. Because the one in whose heart tawheed has been ingrained and deeply rooted, its liveliness will appear in all of his limbs and its tree will give rise to the best of fruits as Allaah, the Exalted, has said:

See you not how Allaah sets forth a parable? A goodly word as a goodly tree, whose root is firmly fixed, and its branches (reach) to the sky. Giving its fruit at all times, by the Leave of its Lord and Allaah sets forth parables for mankind in order that they may remember. [Soorah al-Ibraaheem (14):24~25].

Ibn al-Qayyim said:

"And there is due from the servant to Allaah, in every moment from his time, servitude which will advance him or bring him nearer to Allaah. So if he spends his time in servitude to Allaah, he will advance to his Lord and if he busies himself with desires, or relaxation or inactivity, he will lag behind. And the servant never ceases either to be moving forward or falling behind, and there is no stopping whilst on the path, ever. Allaah, the Exalted, said:

To any of you that chooses to go forward (by working righteous deeds), or to remain behind (by commiting sins). [Soorah al-Muddaththir (74):37]." [Al-Fawaa'id (pp.187~188].

Allaah have mercy on him) from the guidance of the Salaf. Refer to the narrations in this regard in Kitaabuz-Zuhud al-Kabeer of al-Bayhaqee (p.196).

And he (may Allaah have mercy on him) said:

"And if he is not moving forward then he is remaining behind, by necessity. Therefore, the servant is always moving and does never stop (in one place). So either he moves higher or he falls lower, either he moves to the front or he goes to the back ... it is but the steps or phases of a journey which lead, in the most rapid manner, to Paradise or to Hell-fire. Therefore (there is one who is) fast and slow, one who moves forward and one who remains behind and there is no one on the path who stands still, ever. They only differ with each other as to how quickly or slowly they move." [Madaarijus-Saalikeen (1/267)].

I say: The saying of the Prophet (ρ) gives evidence to this,

"All of mankind awake and sells his soul, so (one) either frees it or destroys it," reported by Muslim, and in a version, **"O Ka'b ibn Ujrah! All of mankind awake ..."**[42] so all of them awake (each morning) and whoever does not sell his soul to Allaah, the One who said:

Verily, Allaah has purchased of the believers their lives and their properties, for the price that theirs shall be Paradise. [Soorah at-Tawbah (9):111].

then he has sold it to Satan, the (schemer) who waits in ambush.[43] This is because Allaah has created time for a person and has ordered him with acts of worship which are suitable for the time he has been granted, for it is not so that, **"the acts of worship are greater (more numerous) than the moments of time,"** [44] as

---

[42] Reported by 'Abdur-Razzaaq (20719), Ahmad (3/321), Ibn Hibbaan (7498) and Ibn Hajr declared it authentic in Al-Amaalee al-Mutlaqah (p.214).

[43] Ibn Taymiyyah has indicated this meaning as occurs in Majrnoo'ul-Fataawaa (7/51) and Ibn al-Qayyim in Al-Jawaab al-Kaafee (p.133 of Ar-Riyaan).

[44] In Majmoo'ah Rasaa'il Hasan al-Bannaa, at the end of Risaalatut-Ta'aaleem (p.30). And this phrase, the meaning of which is suspecting and accusing Allaah of oppression, has been made one of the legacies (of advice) of this Imaam, as you can see and it is often distributed in the gatherings of the general-folk. (This is what it is) even though we may be aware that they desire by this to arouse and stimulate the peoples thoughts and concerns for establishing the obligatory aims of the movement! We are not aware of obligations save those of the Sharee'ah, which are facile and

Hasan al-Bannaa has (falsely) claimed, and whoever does not spend his time in what Allaah has commanded, Shaytaan will assault (and ravish) him without respite. Allaah, the Exalted, said:

And recite to them (O Muhammad (ρ)) the story of him to whom We gave Our aayaat (proofs, evidences) but he threw them away. So Satan took control of him, and he became of those who went astray. [Soorah al-Araaf (7):175].

Ibn al-Qayyim said, "(Meaning) that Satan will seize him and keep hold of him in such a manner that he will overcome and attack him, and for this reason He said, **"So Satan took control of him (atba'ahu) ..."** and He did not say, "...followed him (taba'ahu)..." for the meaning of "... took control of him ..." is "... seized and kept hold of him ..." and this is greater than `followed him,' in both wording and meaning." [Al-Fawaa'id (p.100). And refer to the book Madaarikun-Nadhar fis-Siyaasah (pp.390~405) for the completion of this discourse.

---

easy, and all praise is due to Allaah, Who is alone in legislating. And if this was not so and if control of the affair was given to (these such people), they would have burdened us with obligations for which Allaah has sent down no authority!

www.ingramcontent.com/pod-product-compliance
Lightning Source LLC
Chambersburg PA
CBHW051900090426
42811CB00003B/403